The Challenge of
FREE TRADE

The Challenge of
FREE TRADE

Alan Oxley

St. Martin's Press
New York

© Harvester-Wheatsheaf, 1990

All rights reserved. For information, write
Scholarly and Reference Division,
St. Martin's Press, Inc., 175 Fifth Avenue, New York, NY 10010

First published in the United States of America in 1990

Printed in Great Britain

ISBN 0–312–05675–3

Library of Congress Cataloging-in-Publication Data
Applied for.

CONTENTS

Acknowledgements

This book was Mike Moore's idea. It is the direct result of his support and encouragement. Nevertheless the book and the judgements in it are entirely those of the author.

Those who offered helpful comments include Ted Farnon, Barry Martyn, Brian Norwood, and the staff at Harvester Wheatsheaf.

Martin Wolf, David Woods, Gary Banks, Kym Anderson and Richard Blackhurst were kind enough to advise on sources of research and related matters.

Jenny Perry and Ian Stanley helped with word processing and production of the manuscript.

Other contributions were from my family for its perseverance, the dog for relieving the pressure of deadlines by receiving more kicks than its pigheadedness normally warrants and an unusually bad season by the Fitzroy Football club which released time for writing on Saturday afternoons.

Foreword

Alan Oxley's book will be essential reading for anyone with an interest in international trade and its domestic dimensions. For many people the General Agreement on Tariffs and Trade (GATT) can be obscure and difficult to come to terms with. Nevertheless it is the vital element underpinning international trade. The multilateral trading system of rules and disciplines, which has been maintained under the GATT, allowed an extraordinary expansion of global trade and prosperity since the end of the second world war.

Alan Oxley has written in this book a clear guide to the GATT and the international significance of the current round of GATT negotiations. The book is timely. It focuses on the Uruguay Round of trade negotiations, the most complex and ambitious ever undertaken, which is to end in Brussels in December 1990. Alan Oxley has set out, as only an insider could, what the Round is about and what is at stake in these negotiations for all countries. He is forthright and pulls no punches. But he shows no favouritism. He allocates praise and blame where he thinks they fall. He presents a strong case for free trade. His book supports those who believe that further trade liberalization must remain the top objective for all governments involved in the Uruguay Round.

I welcome this book as a landmark in making the GATT better understood by a wide range of non-specialists. I hope it will lead to a greater awareness, especially among all business sectors and consumers throughout the world, of the importance of the current set of trade negotiations.

Now is the time for all those who stand to benefit from the maintenance and expansion of a liberal global trading environment to let their political representative know they support a successful, comprehensive result in the Uruguay Round.

Rt Hon Mike Moore, Prime Minister of New Zealand
September 1990

PROLOGUE

In the third week of September 1986 4,000 ministers, delegates and officials began to arrive at Punta del Este, one of South America's favourite resorts located a hundred kilometres east of Montevideo, for an international trade conference. At some time during the previous 24 hours most would have reflected that they were in the middle of menacing times for international trade.

For the first time since the 1930s powerful elements in the US Congress were flirting with a retreat to protectionism. There was an alarming groundswell of opinion for placing barriers across the board against imports into the United States to prevent the US trade deficit increasing further. An action like this would significantly damage the economy of nearly every country in the world.

The meeting was for trade ministers to decide whether or not to mandate a four-year programme of negotiations to liberalize international trade and revitalize the GATT system of international trade rules. This would be the eighth such meeting since GATT was set up in 1948. Not only was this conference being convened at a critical time: more countries were participating than ever before in the history of the GATT; and the agenda comprised the most complex set of issues ever put before ministers.

The meeting also signalled a preparedness for the first time by developing countries to participate earnestly in international trade liberalization. It was symbolic that, for the first time since the establishment of the GATT forty years before, a conference to launch an international trade negotiation was being held in a developing country. At this stage the ministers were not aware of the momentous changes that were brewing in Europe and what this would mean for the undertaking they were about to launch.

The meeting would not last a week. One of the commendable features of GATT is that its meetings are short. They are for negotiating, not speech making, and a great deal of the pre-negotiating has to be completed before formal meeting are held. The lead up to the Punta meeting had been a two year struggle between those who thought it was time for a global effort to revitalize world trade and those who argued that problems in trade had been caused by the United States and the European Community and that it was their responsibility to fix them. Over the previous decade new forces in international trade had also emerged. This conference and what was to follow from it were going to be unlike any other.

Straws in the wind

The day before the formal opening of the conference US and EC officials met quietly at a pre-arranged venue. Diplomatic protocol and the principle of one country one vote meant that formally every participant had an equal say in the negotiations. However, with a large number of participants this was not practicable and it was an established practice in GATT for the key players to get together quietly outside the formal conference room to 'cut deals'. Such meetings were usually unpublicized and agreements reached in these meetings were fed afterwards into the formal process of negotiations. Some changes to the basic deal were possible but these were invariably minor. The identity of the key players varied from issue to issue. In agriculture the tradition had been for the European Community and the United States to settle the basis of agreement. The Community's officials anticipated that the usual pattern would be followed and that this private meeting would initiate a businesslike, if not necessarily friendly, dialogue.

The EC ministers wanted to start the process of settling the troublesome issue of agriculture. The US discussions were led by Dick Lyng, an elderly and sagacious Secretary of Agriculture. The European Community passed over to the Americans a sheet of paper with some formulations of words designed to straddle the differences between them. The negotiators call this 'language'. Lying spoke sparingly like a New Englander, because of the effects of a stroke a few years before. 'Before we give you a reply to this', he intoned in a low growl, 'I would like to know what the Cairns Group think of it. You should talk to them.' The EC officials were flabbergasted. The Americans were dealing into these private negotiations a ragbag collection of countries which had recently met at a seaside resort in Northern Australia and issued yet another joint declaration of unrealistic demands for free trade in agriculture.

The group comprised nearly all the countries whose cheap agricultural exports faced trade barriers in the European Community, Japan and the United States, and with whom, as a result, the Community had the most vexatious relations. It was also led by the Australians who at the last major GATT conference of ministers four years before had behaved like the Red Guards when they had not got their way on agriculture and stormed out of the meeting. This was the first indication that the Uruguay Round of trade negotiations was not going to be like any other.

The following evening, one of the European Commission's most experienced negotiators joined a group at an enormous party which the Uruguayan government had thrown at the plush, wood panelled Punta del Este Country Club. Unexpectedly, a senior minister from one of the member states turned on him. With all the authority of his office, he publicly dressed the official down for exceeding his brief, undermining the Community's position and acting without authority.

Tensions between the European Commission in Brussels and the member states of the Community were common, but they were usually kept within the Community's four walls. What was behind this extraordinary contretemps? At root was the issue of whether or not services industries such as banking or telecommunications might for the first time be included in

international trade negotiations which had hitherto dealt ex-
clusively with the import and export of goods. This had been a
very controversial question during the preparations for the
conference at Punta. Disagreement had nearly brought the
preparatory process to its knees. India and Brazil, in particular,
were adamant that services had nothing to do with trade or
GATT. The EC ministers, especially the British, wanted services
included in the negotiations. The trade ministers of the EC
member states had met in Brussels a couple of weeks earlier and
agreed that tactically they would line up with the Americans
and others on this issue. The tactic was to isolate India and
Brazil; to make them realize that they were alone on this issue
and that if they continued to hold out they risked the
opprobrium of wrecking the conference.

Some of the member states had discovered that between the
meeting of ministers in Brussels and their arrival in Punta, the
Commission official had been negotiating secretly with India and
Brazil to find an accommodation. This explained the unusual
nature of the public dressing down. Unknown to member states,
the negotiations had been conducted with the authority of
European Commission officials in Brussels. The understanding
achieved – a basis for legally separating negotiations over services
from the negotiations to liberalize trade in goods – ultimately held.
This remarkable train of events pointed to the other major reason
why the Uruguay Round was to be a major ground-breaker.
Services were to be on the agenda for the first time.

In July 1990 at Houston, President Bush surprised his co-
Summiteers when he focussed the Summit on the state of
negotiations in the Uruguay Round with five months to go. The
world saw him challenge President Mitterand, Chancellor Kohl,
Prime Minister Margaret Thatcher and President Delors over the
pace of agricultural reform. In the normal course of events, the
economic reconstruction of Eastern Europe would have topped
the agenda of this summit. It did not because the Uruguay
Round had become high politics. Houston was not the place to
solve the differences, but it focussed attention where it had to be
focussed if the Round were to end successfully five months later
- with the Heads of Government.

While George Bush was putting the Uruguay Round on the table inside the conference room, Fred Bergsten, the Director of the Institute for Ecomonics in Washington was outside sporting a lapel button with the message 'The Uruguay Round is not a dance' This was part of a campaign to introduce the world's media to the Uruguay round. Bergsten had been invited to Houston by Bill Brock, former US Trade Representative and US Senator to moderate a panel discussion for the media about the importance of the Round.

The panel included members of the MTN Coalition – a US business group established to lobby support in the United States for the outcome of the Uruguay Round. It also included members of the Eminent Persons Group on World Trade – an international group of senior figures prominent in international business and government which had been established in April to publicise internationally the importance of the Uruguay Round. Brock was the link. He was co-chairman of the Coalition and one of the originators of the international group.

The international group had been conceived by Mike Moore, the New Zealand Minister for Foreign Relations and Trade, Enrique Iglesias, Managing Director of the Inter-American Bank and former chairman of the ministerial meeting which launched the Uruguay Round, and Brock.

As experienced politicians they all knew that international interest in the Uruguay Round had to be stimulated as it moved to the conclusion of its four-year programme at the end of 1990.

They decided that at the right time in the following year they would invite a group of individuals with significant government or business interests in international trade to collaborate in an international lobbying effort to generate support for the Uruguay Round. The group met in London in April 1990 and chose Otto Graf Lambsdorff, Chairman of the West German Free Democratic Party, Europe's leading free trade politician, as their chairman.

The group included Lord Young, the former UK secretary for trade and industry, and Dr Amnuay Viravan, Chairman of the Bangkok Bank of Thailand and former finance minister, Paul Jolles, Chairman of Nestlé and former chief Swiss trade negotiator, and Peter Sutherland, Chairman of the Allied Irish Bank and former European Commissioner for competition.

Hector Hernandez, Director General of Bancomer and former trade minister of Mexico and Yoshio Okawara, special adviser to Keidanren and former Japanese ambassador to the United States attended the London meeting. Ali Alatas, Indonesia's foreign minister, Paul Volcker, former Chairman of the US Federal Reserve Board, Francois-Xavier Ortoli, Honorary President of Total Petroleum and Ismail Khelil, foreign minister of Tunisia had also agreed to join the group but could not attend the first meeting.

At its first meeting in London, the group declared that failure in the Uruguay Round negotiations could leave chaos and impoverishment as its legacy. It concluded that it was a major international imperative to liberalize international trade and that vigorous international competition was more vital than ever for global growth. The reconstruction of Eastern Europe may have initially overshadowed the importance of the negotiations in the Uruguay Round; but it made success in the negotiations even more important.

The purpose of this book is to analyse what is at stake in the Uruguay Round negotiations. Like the first multilateral trade negotiations in 1948, the Uruguay Round has found itself at one of the crossroads of history. It is one of the great endeavours of modern times. Over one hundred goverments and hundreds of individuals are engaged. Every facet of economic activity around the globe could be affected by some aspect of the outcome. International agreement to apply afresh the precepts of open international trade arrangements would influence dramatically patterns of global growth in the next century. The opportunity exists

1. To increase global growth.
2. To break the developing country debt cycle.
3. To increase global food production.
4. To underpin economic and political renewal in Eastern Europe.
5. To prevent a slide into inefficient trading blocs.
6. To apply the dynamism of the information age to expand global trade.

The Uruguay Round presents the challenge of free trade.

Part One

THE CHANGING GLOBAL ECONOMY

Chapter One

THE WORLD FROM WHICH GATT AROSE

A re-ordering world

The GATT (General Agreement on Tariffs and Trade) system of multilateral trade arrangements was part of the scheme to restructure international relations after the Second World War. GATT was built on the political and economic order of Europe as determined by the Yalta accords. It reflected the Atlantic order of things. The dominant members of GATT were the Western and North American democratic market economies. International trade was dominated by the United States.

It is worth recalling the features of the world in 1950 to recall the environment out of which GATT arose. The United States was the unchallenged military and economic superpower; the trans-Atlantic axis was Washington–London; Western Europe was being economically reconstructed through the Marshall Plan; the cold war and the division of Europe became institutionalized; and economic growth was an instrument in that war. Japan's GDP was still below pre-war levels.

The purpose of GATT was to persuade signatories to commit themselves to liberal trading principles and to lock into arrangements which progressively pegged their economies to international market prices. The fundamental principle was that open markets were the most efficient and the operating premise was that measures which impeded trade should have the least distorting effect on markets and should be gradually reduced.

The history – a patchwork

GATT's history is well known. It emerged from joint planning between the Americans and the British during the last years of the Second World War for the structure of international economic relations after the War. The aim was to prevent a return to the chaos of protectionism in the 1930s.

In 1929 the United States dominated the world economy. It produced about 45 per cent of the world's manufactures and accounted for 20 per cent of global exports. Imposition of tariffs by the United States through the notorious Smoot–Hawley Act in 1930 and then imposition of trade barriers by others, especially the United Kingdom, saw the volume in trade of manufactures fall by 40 per cent by the end of 1932. The average level of the US tariff after Smoot–Hawley rose from 38 per cent to 53 per cent.

The period at the end of the Second World War was marked by idealism and commitments to internationalism. For a short time these factors tempered the normal influence of realpolitik in international relations. Post-war plans to construct a new international order were ambitious. As well as the United Nations the plans included an International Monetary Fund, a World Bank and an International Trade Organization.

The details of the trade organization were negotiated between 1946 and 1948. The objective was to prevent the spiralling falls in trade flows and growth that escalating closures of markets had caused in the 1930s. The economic mismanagement of the 1930s was widely regarded as one of the primary contributors to the instability which led to the outbreak of World War II. The US Congress killed the International Trade Organization and the General Agreement on Tariffs and Trade, which was to have been an interim and subordinate component of the ITO, was all that survived. GATT began in 1947 with 23 signatories of which the majority were developed countries. Its rationale was simple although the *modus operandi* was complicated.

International rules

The basic reason for transferring sovereignty to an international organization is a noble one: it is to accept the application of an international standard in place of national and more parochial interests. The second half of the twentieth century is the most internationalist period in human history. But commitments to internationalism are still not strong. In most countries conflicts between domestic and international interests are usually resolved in a way that takes more account of domestic interests.

When they sign GATT governments surrender the freedom to regulate trade, particularly imports, and accept international rules in its place. Most countries join GATT because the government of the day has decided that the commitments to liberalize trade which are inherent in membership are in the interests of the national economy. They therefore use the international commitments of GATT to support actions to open up their national economies and counter the arguments of those who oppose liberalization.

This is a reasonable deal. Most interests opposed to change enjoy some form of economic benefit which has been conferred by regulation. They may have the sole right to an import licence or may share this right with only a few others. It is interesting to observe in countries where import licences are common how many are held by cronies or relatives of those in power, or the military. Whatever the origin of the granting of the licence the holder is likely to be wealthy and have influence.

It is often helpful, and usually effective, particularly in a small country, for the authorities to be able to counter this type of influence by pointing to solemn international legal obligations to do it differently. Even government authorities in large and powerful countries sometimes find it useful to invoke GATT rules to advance a change or argue against a particular proposal for financial assistance for industry.

The limited extent of commitment to international sovereignty means that the success of international agreements depends fundamentally on the extent to which the most powerful signatories to those agreements are prepared to support them. The rules may not appear to recognize different levels of influence but the more powerful members of any international system of rules have a disproportionate say in the maintenance of the credibility of those rules. In 1950 that influence was enjoyed by the United States and to a lesser extent by Britain and France. Today, it is enjoyed by the United States and the European Community and increasingly by Japan.

When acceding to GATT countries commit themselves to certain rules, such as using tariffs only for protection. They also agree that any reduction in a tariff negotiated with one party will also extend to all other parties. And they commit themselves to participate in regular negotiations to reduce tariffs.

After 1948 a two-part process emerged fairly quickly. On the one hand was the day to day operation of the Agreement. A key part of this were the dispute procedures where one party could ask for adjudication over a breach of GATT rights by another party. On the other hand, were the major conferences where the parties would come together for the sole purpose of negotiating to reduce tariffs. These became known as the rounds of trade negotiations.

There have been seven rounds of negotiations since GATT began in 1948 (see Table 1.1). The Uruguay Round is the eighth. The United States has driven the pattern of conferences to reduce trade barriers. The timing of the conferences was originally dictated by the timing of successive renewals by Congress of the administration's mandate to negotiate tariff reductions.

The procedures to negotiate reductions of tariffs were cleverly designed to build in a momentum for liberalization. The operating principle was that tariff reductions should not be

TABLE 1.1 *Trade rounds: sessions of multilateral trade negotiations*

1947	Geneva
1949	Annecy (France)
1950–51	Torquay (UK)
1956	Geneva
1960–62	Dillon Round (Geneva)
1964	Kennedy Round (Geneva)
1974–79	Tokyo Round (Geneva – launched Tokyo)
1986–89	Uruguay Round (Geneva – launched Punta del Este)

reversible. Once two parties agreed to a package to lower tariffs these agreements were recorded in a tariff schedule. Whenever a party wanted to raise one of those tariffs it was obliged to go to the party with which the tariff reduction had been originally agreed, as well as to other principal suppliers of the product concerned, and offer to negotiate to compensate for trade lost through the raising of the tariff. Usually the offer was to lower a tariff on some other product.

The rules also required that any lowering of a tariff had to be extended to all other parties. Trade rounds created their own momentum for liberalization. With all major traders participating simultaneously in a negotiation to lower tariffs this stimulated the optimal amount of liberalization.

Exceptions to the rules

The system had major imperfections from the outset. France and the United Kingdom wanted to preserve the systems of imposing lower tariffs on imports from their colonies and to exclude these tariffs from the GATT rule that the same tariff level should be applied to all parties. When the European Community was formed a decade later it maintained the effective exclusion from the non-discriminatory principles of GATT of the special levels of tariffs which offered access on preferential terms to exports from the former colonies of the member states. This arrangement became the Lomé Convention.

Another major exemption was allowed to the rule that quotas were not permitted as a means of restricting trade (only tariffs were allowed). Quotas were allowed on imports of agricultural products in special circumstances, thus beginning a long history of not applying basic GATT rules to trade in agricultural products. In 1955 the United States created a further exception for agriculture. It secured the right not to apply GATT rules to a substantial part of the agricultural produce imported into the United States. It was then the largest agricultural trading nation and this action contributed significantly to the principle that GATT rules could not apply *in toto* to agriculture.

Japan joined GATT in 1955 but a number of countries reserved their rights not to accord Japan full rights under GATT so that quotas which discriminated against Japanese products could be kept in place. A major concern was exports of cheap Japanese textiles. Within a few years developing countries were also becoming uncomfortably competitive in textiles and in 1961 a 'Short Term Arrangement' was agreed. This was to operate for one year. It allowed industrialized countries to impose individual quotas on imports of textiles from developing countries. This agreement contravened two key GATT principles. First, it allowed quotas rather than tariffs to be used. Second, it allowed trade barriers which discriminated between various parties.

The European Community formed in 1958. While individual members of the Community remained independent parties to GATT, over time the European Commission came to represent them in GATT proceedings. The impact of the Community on GATT was large. The initial effect was that the effective exclusion of agriculture from GATT disciplines was consolidated. The Common Agricultural Policy (CAP) was one of the key instruments of the Community, and the Community was not about to allow liberal trade principles to apply to it.

By 1960 GATT had 37 contracting parties, the majority of which were still industrialized countries. As time progressed the practice of excluding competitive products from the scope of the Agreement developed. The short term arrangement on textiles was replaced within a year by the 'Long Term Arrangement', which certainly became that. Initially it was to last for four years. It was extended to cover also products which were 50 per cent cotton. As a form of counterbalance the Arrangement offered developing country exporters an annual growth in the volume of exports of 5 per cent.

The Arrangement was progressively expanded to encompass more products each time a new one looked like threatening some part of trade in the United States or the European Community. In 1974 the restrictions were extended to all wool, cotton and synthetic fibres. It became the Multi-Fibre Arrangement (MFA). Its rules were more complex and restrictive but the basic figure of annual growth of exports was lifted to 6 per cent. The amount of trade which could be conducted in open markets according to the most competitive price shrank further.

Another exception to GATT rules was created in 1971. GATT parties agreed that countries could lower tariffs on imports from developing countries and not be obliged to extend those same lower tariffs to all imports. This was to allow lower tariff rates to be extended to exports from developing countries in accordance with a Generalized System of Preferences (GSP) which had been developed in the UN Conference on Trade and Development (UNCTAD) a few years before. This accorded with the prevailing philosophy among developing countries at the time that they could not compete with developed countries and deserved special preference. These arrangements did not result in a significant shift of trade outside GATT rules.

Successful liberalization

In the areas where GATT trading principles have been allowed to function, primarily in the trade of manufactures, the system has been successful. The volume of world trade multiplied nine times between 1946 and 1985. In the 1950s and 1960s, the volume of trade increased at double the rate of growth of output and income (see Figure 1.1). In the post-war period growth in trade has on average been greater than growth in output.

By the early 1970s, after tariffs had been cut to the levels negotiated in the Kennedy Round of trade negotiations, economists estimated that the average tariff for manufactured goods was just over 9 per cent. The reductions negotiated in the Tokyo Round brought tariffs down even further – the averages were 4.9 per cent in the United States, 6.0 per cent in the European Community and 5.4 per cent in Japan. The GATT rules for liberalization of world trade had significantly contributed to this.

This pattern of growth was not even across all sectors of trade or among all countries, however. Most of this trade was among the industrialized countries. The terms of trade for agricultural and other primary products fell. Trade barriers were constructed against the exports of developing countries, especially textiles and also against processed rather than raw products. The global trade share of the Eastern European countries fell.

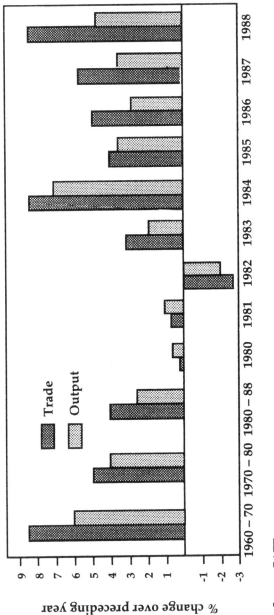

FIGURE 1.1 *Growth in world trade and output*

Source: GATT

Expanding exceptions

Towards the end of the 1960s, the United States instituted a practice of placing restrictions on the import of items which were too competitively priced for domestic producers, but by methods which avoided GATT disciplines. US steel producers were facing steep competition from more efficient Japanese exporters. Their supporters in Congress prepared a bill proposing severe import restrictions which would have been illegal under GATT.

The inducement of not facing the restrictions which were in the Congressional bill and concern not to be seen as a trouble maker in the US market encouraged the major Japanese steel exporters to introduce 'voluntary' export restraints, the terms of which were negotiated with the United States and the European Community. The Community also went along with this arrangement, although since the EC was not as low cost a producer as Japan the arrangement did not restrain EC exports to the same extent. This proved to be a convenient arrangement for the US and EC. It was renewed for steel trade in the early 1970s.

As the United States and European Community faced challenges from cheaper exports from Japan, as well as from Korea and Taiwan, they pressured exporters to resort increasingly to the use of grey area measures like voluntary restraint arrangements. They were applied to exports of foot-wear, electronic goods, cars and machine tools. GATT did not explicitly rule these measures out. They were certainly contrary to the economic principles which underpined GATT but until tested in the GATT judicial arena no one could say they were illegal: they were a 'grey area'.

But the United States and the European Community avoided GATT safeguards which did allow temporary barriers to be put in place against sudden surges of imports. The rules assumed that the measures would be temporary until the domestic industry had been restructured. The country whose imports had been cut back was entitled to some form of compensation, most probably increased access for some other product. And the restrictions had to apply to the product, not the country of origin.

The United States and the European Community were simply

not prepared to operate under these strictures. They were either unprepared or considered themselves unable to face up to the companies and unions which would have born the brunt of restructuring. It is now a generally accepted view that through the 1960s most of the OECD countries overemphasized the development of social security structures which encouraged rigidity in the labour force. This compounded the difficulties they faced when oil prices were hiked in the 1970s.

Tariffs had been reduced but to an extent they had become much less important trade barriers. New non-tariff barriers (NTBs) were now a major problem. As a result the Tokyo Round of international trade negotiations which ran from 1973 to 1979 focused as much on non-tariff barriers as tariff barriers.

The Atlantic hangover

The GATT open trading system now effectively applies to trade in manufactures and supports an active trade among the industrialized countries . These markets are basically open to all exporters and importers. Even within this sector there are some very significant exceptions. Motor vehicles account for a very high percentage of the exports of the traditional big exporters. Yet this is an area of trade which the United States and the European Community have effectively removed from the liberal trading system. New exporters may enter the motor vehicle markets in the European Community and the United States only if they are not too competitive.

It could be said, therefore, that an unwritten law underpins GATT. Its principles are given full application where the trade in question complements and does not threaten the current patterns of trade among the trans-Atlantic industrialized countries. Japan is not a full participant in this consensus – in fact it has been the first victim of it. The techniques pioneered to contain Japanese competitiveness have also been employed against the newly industrializing countries.

Global growth patterns have changed significantly since Yalta. Trans-Atlantic trade is important but it does not dominate global trade as it did in the early 1950s. Trans-Pacific and Pacific–Atlantic trade patterns are not properly catered for by the GATT trading system. The Uruguay Round is a further evolution in the process of extending the traditional focus of international trade negotiations away from tariffs to other barriers to trade. As GATT disciplines are extended to those areas neglected patterns and sectors of trade will be embraced.

GATT's foundations were the political accords which emerged from Yalta and the trans-Atlantic economic trading system which was constructed at Bretton Woods. Mikhail Gorbachev began the unravelling of the political framework of this order in 1989. The economic order has been unravelling for two decades. The success of the Uruguay Round will be the success that the European Community and the United States allow it to be. While its success is in their hands a number of other players have strong interests in the re-invigoration of the multilateral trading system and the extension of its benefits to more countries.

Chapter Two

THE WORLD FACING GATT

When the Uruguay Round concludes at the end of 1990 those participating will be at one of the crossroads of history. Several fundamental changes will be underway.

1. The underpinnings of international relations among the states of Europe will have been re-ordered.

2. The management of international relations among the most powerful countries in the world will for the first time in nearly half a century not be based on military alliances but will instead be shaped by economic interests and, in the case of the Europeans, economic obligations.

3. International business will be evaluating whether its global interests will be best served by being competitive or by cooperating with the competition.

4. Information technology will be laying the basis for acceleration of the efficiency of international commercial transactions and will globalize markets further.

In addition, governments will have the opportunity to address issues which will be fundamental to global economic growth over the next decade and into the next century.

1. Improving global food production.

2. Providing a strong basis for economic growth among many developing countries.

3. Underpinning the introduction of market economies in Eastern Europe.
4. Providing a basis for global competition and competitiveness.

GATT has been an effective but imperfect instrument. But it has been tailored to suit the interests of economies which have an established trade in manufactures. Without change it cannot serve the interests of those countries which trade in commodities or textiles; it is not able to operate to meet the interests of the new growth economies in the Pacific; and it cannot support the new forces of competitive and information technology-based services which will increasingly drive global trade in the future.

Challenges to Europe – temptation of the Middle Kingdom

The coincidence of the Single Market and the reunification of Germany now offer the most dramatic advance in European integration since the European Economic Community was set up in 1958. Economic and monetary integration of the EC countries will challenge Europeans to think about their interests in an open, global trading system and how they will participate in future in the global economy.

Fears that the Single Market would lead to 'Fortress Europe' have abated, although some harbour suspicions that a 'capital' fortress rather than a 'trade' fortress is emerging. The price for participating in the new, less regulated markets of the Community may not be crossing a trade barrier but investing in Europe on regulated terms. This approach started to characterize the Community's attitude towards Japan's trade and investment in the late 1980s.

Since the formation of the European Community there has always been a tension in economic and trade policy between the interests that arise from looking inward and outward. Key members of the Community such as France and Italy have always been ambivalent about open trade and the importance of the GATT trading system. Community obligations to open markets among member states have commanded more weight than obligations under GATT to remove barriers between the Community as a whole and the rest of the world. On the whole the Community has made GATT accommodate to its regulations and requirements as much as it has accommodated to them itself.

This is understandable. A great deal of the trade of the European Community is not conducted on the basis of open, global competition which GATT is designed to foster. About half of the trade of EC member states is with other member states. The major instrument of the Community, the CAP, which absorbs more than half of the budget of the European Community, is protectionist. And the greater part of the relations between the Community and its other trading partners is conducted through arrangements which give access to the Community's markets on preferred terms. The European Community has such arrangements with the EFTA countries, North African countries, the developing countries which are members of the Lomé Convention, and now with the Eastern European countries.

Great pressures to turn the focus of the attention of Europe inward are building. An enormous change has occurred. International relations in Europe will be determined by economic obligations not military alliances. The European Commission is now more important than NATO. Management of a common currency will have a greater effect on the United Kingdom than the location of British Army units in Germany. The framework for examining issues has become more European than before.

The single market programme drove the EFTA countries to seek closer association with the European Community. The free market aspirants in Eastern Europe seek this as well. The single market and economic integration will encourage pan-EC business operations and the sharpening of the focus of European business on the European continent. If the prospect is not an investment fortress Europe it may be a European Middle Kingdom which has its back turned on the rest of the world.

The attitudes in the European business world towards competitiveness will be a basic influence. Increased competitiveness was one of the goals of the European Commission architects of the single market. It is likely to have three effects. Small and medium sized businesses will expand and combine to exploit the pan-European markets. Large businesses will be challenged to form truly pan-European conglomerates which are globally competitive: 'national champions' will have to go. This will test the commitments of member-states to pan-Europeanism. If European business conglomerates that are globally competitive do not emerge one of the central objectives of the Single Market, which was to stimulate emergence of large European companies, will not be achieved.

The largest European businesses will face the challenge of how to maintain or secure a place in the increasingly globalized international markets. In some industries American and particularly Japanese competition has been fierce. The options are to match it, to drive it out or to collaborate with it. In the long term the only effective approach is to match it. The alternative of collaboration has lately become particularly fashionable under the guise of forging strategic alliances. There is no one definition of what a strategic alliance is, but the form of it which would most run against the interests of open trading arrangements is the cartel. Cartels have always demonstrated that profits and economic efficiency are not synonymous.

The extension across continental Europe of a general economic and trading system in which there is an inclination to turn the back on the rest of the world could mesh with a more calculated interest to protect European industry from competitive pressures from outside Europe, especially East Asia. Increasing use of anti-dumping procedures to protect EC industry against competitive imports and the imposing of rules for high local content of products and conditions for investment show the existence of such inclinations. There may be an attempt to justify protection from pressure outside Europe on the grounds that this was reasonable compensation for accepting adjustment to greater internal competition with the creation of the Single Market.

There will be other pressures in other directions. A number of key European businesses have distinct global interests. Some have deliberately maintained a strong international presence outside Europe because of this. They appreciate that if they reduce exposure to the most competitive segments of the international market in East Asia and the United States then they are sowing the seeds for long term decline. The importance of maintaining competition is also appreciated in the European

Commission, which has in recent years demonstrated determination to enforce EC competition laws. A number of large collusive arrangements and government subsidies to particular industries have had to be undone because of Commission pressure.

Many firms appreciate the importance of liberalization and deregulation of the services sectors if profitability and efficiency is to be achieved. The Single Market will open up some of these sectors, especially the financial sector, in Europe. International financial markets are already global and major efficiencies are to be achieved through global deregulation of financial and telecommunication markets. European companies with global business have a major interest in seeing this happen.

The agricultural sector, Europe's most protected, is also facing major change. There will be heavy demands on Western Europe's governments to finance the reconstruction of Eastern Europe. Pressure will mount to direct existing funds in the Commission budget to Eastern Europe and away from existing programmes, the largest of which is the CAP.

Given the falling farm population in Europe, especially in France and Germany, it will be increasingly difficult to mount a case for maintaining such high levels of support. Interest in allowing the market to influence the character of agricultural production in the Community will grow among the policy makers. Concern to reduce the polluting side effects of agriculture in Europe will also generate pressure to reduce production. Altering farming methods to reduce pollution is expensive. If production is not cut, the costs to government will escalate even further.

The United States – the two-headed abstract figure

The national debate over protection or open markets in the United States throughout the 1980s reflects the point to which the GATT trading system has evolved. The United States has concurrently followed policies of protection and free trade. It is like one of Picasso's figures where two profiles of the same face look at each other on the same head.

The debate in the United States will continue on two planes. There is the straightforward debate between those who want protection, such as those in the textile and steel industries, and those who oppose it, like the international financial services companies. The other plane is more complex and relates to the basic budgetary problems and the budget deficit of the US government. Debate about the consequences of these policies has been conducted in the language of trade problems. The manifestation of the problem is being treated as the symptom.

This has been complicated by attitudes towards Japan. While the US imbalance of trade with Japan is not so different from that with Germany, Japan's profile is different. The Japanese are formidable competitors and have successfully assaulted significant, highly visible markets in the United States, such as consumer electronics and automobiles. Their business perspective is long term and they are a different style of competitor from that to which US industry is accustomed. Finally, their domestic markets have been closed and they have recently become significant and high profile investors in the United States, although they are not the largest foreign investor. In short, the Japanese 'problem' is a manifestation of macroeconomic policies and has been a continuing political problem for successive administrations. This situation will continue into the 1990s.

The Bush administration has shown an inclination to reduce protection. It resisted pressure from the steel industry in 1989 to renew steel quotas for five years, instead introducing a shorter-term quota with an invitation to other exporters to act collectively to liberalize international trade in steel. It has supported strongly the Uruguay Round. It has also resisted a number of more extreme pressures from Congress to put pressure on Japan. But until the US budget deficit is brought under control it will continue to face domestic pressure to constrain cheaper imports from Japan and the other competitive East Asian economies.

Two other pressures will drive US attitudes. There is a long-term trend towards freer trading arrangements in the Western hemisphere. The free trade agreement between the United States and Canada will have a significant effect. Most tariffs on manufactured goods shipped between the two countries will be removed over a ten-year period. Most of Canada's trade is with the United States and GATT will become much less important to Canada. The United States has committed to negotiate a free trade arrangement with Mexico. This will be driven by geo-political concerns and business interests. Very significant large-scale investment in manufacturing is being made in Mexico by US companies to supply global and US markets. These companies will exert pressure for trade barriers between the two markets to be lowered.

The idea of a free trade bloc in the North American continent is a formidable one. The disparities between the United States and Mexican economies are so large that the elimination of all trade barriers between the United States and Mexico will not be feasible for ten to twenty years. Progressive development of preferential trading arrangements between them can be expected, however. The general concept of a free trade bloc comprising Canada, the United States and Mexico as part of a network of free trade arrangements around the world, with the United States at the middle, is seen as an alternative to a global trading system, particularly if a greater Europe is turned in on itself. Before the Reagan administration committed itself fully to the Uruguay Round it held out a network of free trade arrangements as an alternative, long-term objective.

The second pressure arises from the success experienced from pressuring countries bilaterally to open their markets. Congress has discovered that applying bilateral pressure to secure access for a US product can work, especially if the country concerned has a range of bilateral interests with the United States. While the administration has in the past sought to justify using this approach on the grounds that others did not secure access, it will be difficult to get rid of this practice; it is likely to be exercised whenever Congress enjoys a preponderant influence over the administration.

The junking of revolutionary expansionist communist ideology by the Soviet Union will mark the beginning of US military disengagement from Europe. The US perspective on the Pacific will sharpen and the area will become a forum for competition for influence between the United States and Japan. This competition will range from friendly to acrimonious. US judgements about how it sees its role in the region will influence what shape international trading arrangements will take. On balance it is likely that US/Japanese economic cooperation will strengthen overall. The common interest to be achieved through this is too great to ignore. It would represent a confluence of two cultures which have never been afraid to adapt the best from elsewhere. The United States would also consider it to be in its interest that the growing economies of East Asia develop open market economies. These countries will be major US trading partners and important targets for US investment.

The United States has significant trade and investment interests in Latin America. US banks are heavily exposed to the Latin American debt overhang. Latin American markets were important for US exports but their need to service debt has reduced their capacity to import. The result is that the debt crisis has made its own contribution to the US trade imbalance. There is growing recognition in the United States that a key part of the strategy of dealing with the debt problem will be to enable the countries concerned to trade out of it. This will require markets to be opened.

The US administration and the more farsighted US farm leaders perceive that protection and manipulation of global agricultural markets fundamentally undermines the US agricultural industry. US farm leaders know that US agriculture will not achieve global competitiveness until it is driven basically by market forces. Disputes with the European Community over access to markets has been a running sore for years. Until international rules are agreed which begin to let the market have some say in international agricultural trade major problems will continue. The issue will be a continuing source of friction between the United States and the Community.

Major US companies are at the leading edge of the internationalization of the global economy. Their prospects for growth are tied to the fortunes of the global economy and more and more of them are fixing on what is necessary to make the global economy function better. This is why liberalization of the services sector is such an important objective for them. The largest, most efficient player in any system always gains the greatest benefit when encouraging liberalization because it encourages others to open markets. But the interest of the big US services companies is wider than this. A number of these companies have become global companies and see the global economy as a single unit.

Eastern Europe – avoiding old wine in new bottles

The economies of Eastern Europe were removed from the global market economy by the Soviet Union in the late 1940s. It created the Eastern bloc economic system – Comecon – which bound the Soviet's satellites to trade with it and each other in an international version of the command economy. Levels of trade and prices were bartered and negotiated. Integration of the Eastern European economies into GATT global trading arrangements was not practicable. Most of the Eastern European countries joined GATT, but on special terms.

The question most commonly asked about how the centrally planned economies of Eastern Europe operated in the GATT market system was how could one determine if their exports were being dumped. The GATT system operated on the basis of prices set by the market. In the centrally planned economies prices were set artificially. Sometimes the terms of accession for these economies set targets for annual increases in imports as a means of artificially stimulating greater trade performance. This was an abrogation from GATT principles, but given that the trade involved was limited it did not matter so much. The USSR was the biggest trader in Eastern Europe but it was not a member of GATT.

All the Eastern European governments have set themselves on the difficult task of converting their economies to market economies. There is little point in their replacing industries which were inefficient in a command economy with industries which will be inefficient in a market economy. As the economies reconstruct the goal will be to introduce international standards of efficiency into production. To succeed they must be able to trade into foreign markets and open their own markets to trade. They are all now looking for GATT rules to reinforce the difficult transition and to provide pressure to keep international markets open.

If the international environment within which Eastern European countries develop domestic market mechanisms is not open they will not be able to attain global standards of competitiveness. In these circumstances the Eastern Europeans will be at the mercy of whatever markets will be open be to them. It would be a tragedy if efficient modes of agricultural production, such as in Hungary, or the modes of production in new, rebuilt steel industries, were adjusted to operate at the average level of inefficiency of EC industry simply because the European Community was the only market available. The extent to which the industrialized world liberalizes its own economies will have a direct bearing on the capacity of governments in Eastern Europe to introduce effective market mechanisms.

The Third World – the search for growth

The Third World presents a mixed picture. There has been spectacular success, especially among the East Asian economies. Within a decade – sooner for some – they will have the full attributes of industrialized countries. The situation of these countries today may be compared to that of the democracies of Europe immediately after the Second World War. Their economies are not devastated, but for sustained growth they need an open international trading system and need to be encouraged to liberalize their own economies. They are demonstrating readiness to lower trade barriers and liberalize. Some face the choice now which faced Japan in the 1960s of basing continuing growth on exports and restricting access to domestic markets or of integrating their economies fully into an open international trading system.

Others face the economic oppression of the debt burden. These countries are now transferring net resources to the industrialized world. The economic situation in some Latin American countries has led them to verge on the edge of chaos and social collapse. While the primary action to correct the fundamentals in their economies has to be taken by these countries themselves, if there are not markets for them to trade into their basic problems will be almost impossible to correct. The two most heavily protected markets in the industrialized world, agriculture and textiles, are the ones in which developing countries enjoy competitive advantage and the greatest trading opportunities.

Opening agricultural markets would provide ready markets for the debt burdened Latin Americans. Global liberalization of the agricultural sector would also be an important potential stimulant of growth in many developing countries. This was the experience in Thailand and China where increasing agricultural production was one of the engines of development. As well as generating growth in the economy it obviously increases food production. A global increase in food production will be necessary over the next decade. There will be improvements in productivity from new technology. But improvement in the economic climate for food production – liberalization of international markets and liberalization of arrangements governing production and distribution in developing countries — will have the most effect. There is a direct link between excess production and protection of agriculture in Europe, the United States and Japan, and the solution to the debt problem and improvement of global food production.

The textile, and particularly clothing industry, in the developing countries could also contribute substantially to growth in the developing countries if markets in the industrialized world were opened. The countries that would benefit most – China, India, Pakistan and Bangladesh – are also some of those that will experience the most significant population growth by the end of the century. These countries need increased trade opportunities upon which to base growth.

Japan and the Pacific century

Before the lowering of the Iron Curtain directed attention to Europe strategic analysts were focusing on the long term place of the Pacific in global development. The twenty-first century was being described as the 'Pacific century'. The fascination with this idea derived from the economic synergy achievable from the combinations of trans-Pacific trade and investment involving Japan, the newly industrializing economies (NIEs) – South Korea, Taiwan, and Hong Kong, the United States and Canada, the ASEAN countries (Singapore, Malaysia, Thailand, the

Philippines, Indonesia and Brunei), Australia and New Zealand and a steadily growing China. Extraordinary combinations of markets, resources, capital and technology can be contemplated from this assemblage. It remains probable that from these synergies will emerge the primary stimulants for global competitiveness and growth over the next quarter century.

Japan's role will be critical. It will continue to be a dominant, global economic power. Japanese industry has set new international standards of competitiveness and it will strive for leadership in all fields of high technology. Japanese companies, like US companies, are developing global conceptions of international markets. These companies are now transferring their skills and technology to other countries. This will develop further as Japanese investment in manufacturing in Europe and the United States increases. Unless other factors such as xenophobia come into play a Nissan produced in the United Kingdom will soon be as European as a Ford Scorpio.

Japan has the capacity to depress global growth as well as to stimulate it. In Japan there is a strong spirit of competition but not a deep philosophical commitment to the economics of open markets. At times Japanese industry does engage in anti-competitive predatory pricing and capture of markets. Japanese industry is accustomed to taking direction from government and it is not surprising that it has been such a willing accomplice in arrangements proposed by the Americans and the Europeans to manage levels of trade.

Japan has continued to direct its motor vehicle exporters to restrain the number of cars they export to the United States long after the US administration has ceased asking it to do so. Japan has started to direct its importers to increase the level of imports from designated countries in order to reduce Japan's trade imbalances. Jagdish Bhagwati of Columbia University, one of the great modern academics on trade economics, has coined the term 'voluntary import expansions' to describe this phenomenon. Tax incentives are now available to Japanese companies which reach specific targets for imports. The Japanese government is subsidizing imports.

To its credit Japan has responded to pressures to liberalize its economy and support an open, global trading system. As Japan's preponderance as a global trader grows in key sectors the extent of Japanese commitment to liberal, global trading arrangements will be one of the determinants of the international vitality of that system. There is scope for leadership by Japan. If Japan does not exercise leadership and continues to participate in managed trade arrangements, the responsibility will remain primarily with the European Community and the United States to encourage Japan to support an open rather than managed trading system. Whether they can do so credibly is another matter.

The drive from the Asian/Pacific economies is what will keep growth rates and levels of efficiency higher in the Pacific than anywhere else in the world. Over the next decade growth in Japan is likely to be higher than the average among OECD countries. The rate of growth among the NIEs is likely to be less than that experienced during the last decade but still higher than that in Japan; and the average rate of growth among the ASEAN countries is expected to be higher than for any other region over the next decade. China will be slow to recover from the overheating and runaway growth of the first half of the 1980s, but another spurt should be expected in the second half of the 1990s.

More than any other aggregation of economies these economies have pegged their economic development to growth in trade. The issue in the region will be growth. Their ability to grow will depend on major markets being kept open. The trade and economic interests of the NIEs are at something of a crossroad. Their basic interest would be best served by an open, global system. However, there are forces inclining them to examine economic cooperation within the region.

The primary markets of the NIEs and the ASEAN countries are the United States, Japan and the rest of the region. They have been in the strategic orbit of the United States for the last half century and are comfortable with that. Japanese trade and particularly investment through the region constitutes another common thread. The progressive erection of barriers and use of administrative procedures by the European Community to exports of manufactures and commodities from the Asia/Pacific region has created the perception that the Community is either disinterested in the region or antipathetic to it. The Asia/Pacific exporters have been bruised by pressure from the United States, but on balance its markets have remained open. Governments in the region know that a global, liberal trading system is the best for them. However, if the GATT system is not improved to meet their interests, they will be tempted to look to other possibilities.

Chapter Three

THE TRADE CHALLENGES OF THE 1990s AND BEYOND –
development, debt and food

The 1990s present mixed prospects for developing countries. Some developing countries in the Asia/Pacific area foresee living standards on a par with the industrialized countries. For most of Latin America the battle will be to reverse declining or stagnating living standards; in many parts of Africa the basis for economic viability has yet to be established; and in continental Asia, as well as North Africa, the challenge will be to lift economic growth above population growth. The world's population will increase and so will the demand for food.

The problems are diverse, as are the solutions. Better access to the markets of industrialized economies will not solve all the problems. In some areas, however, protection of important markets is a fundamental hindrance to economic growth in developing countries. Markets in the industrialized world are closed to products which are efficiently produced in the developing world in order to sustain and support inefficient and frequently rich producers.

Because the effects are often indirect, and sometimes because the economics are not understood, linkages between strangled growth opportunities and protection of industry in the industrialized and developing worlds are frequently not perceived. Division of the world into blocs – the Third World, (neither East nor West) and the North and the South has tended to obscure some of these linkages.

The North/South divide crumbles

Like the 'East-West' divide in Europe, the underpinnings of the concepts Third World and non-alignment are being swept away by the reconstruction of the political order of Europe. Even the idea of the 'Third World' is no longer valid. It was conceived as next after the 'First' of the capitalist world and the 'Second' of the Communist world. The Non-Aligned Movement was the international political arm of the Third World through which Nasser, Nehru, Tito and Soekarno found common comfort and defence against the blandishments of Washington and Moscow to side against the other during the cold war. They are no longer asked to take sides.

The neat categorization of the rich 'North' and the poor 'South' is also losing credibility. The economies of Spain and Portugal had always had some features more common to the developing world than to the rich North; and Turkey and Yugoslavia sat in a no man's land between North and South. These were manageable exceptions. But as the economies of Eastern Europe gravitate from the East to the North the exceptions enlarge to become established features. Most Eastern European countries have now been recognized as 'developing' countries at least for the purpose of the preferential access to markets which is available to developing countries. The diffusion of the dichotomy is mirrored in the South with the emergence of South Korea, Taiwan, Singapore and Hong Kong where standards of living are higher than in the developing parts of the North.

As the North/South divide crumbles at the edges the simplicity of the case for the North assisting the South, as well as the morality of it which used to be taken for granted, starts to diminish. Alarm has been expressed in parts of Africa that resources for which Third World development used to have first claim are being diverted to reconstruct Eastern Europe. Perhaps this is good. It will require a re-examination of the problems of development to see how they might be addressed if less financial assistance is available. A second effect of the blurring of the borders between North and the South is that economic problems which are common to nearly all economic systems, regardless of their levels of sophistication, will be more clearly seen as such.

Development problems

While the blurring of the North/South dichotomy may assist analysis of problems and development of solutions this is not to say that problems of development do not exist or are diminished. There are three major problems. The first is the challenge in key parts of the world to raise living standards in the face of continuing population growth. The answer to this problem lies in two spheres – improving economic growth and reducing population growth. The second key issue is to secure growth in a form in which the environment is sustained, not only for its own sake but as a continuing source of support for human activity. The third problem is to achieve continuous economic growth.

Changing responses

The lessons of the three decades of experience since Europe's colonial empires were dismantled is that the broad prescriptions for improving the welfare of the developing world which were adopted in the 1960s and 1970s have on the whole not worked. The presumption was that developing countries at large could not industrialize to compete with the West and that their fundamental reliance on exports of commodities would continue. This perspective fitted in with a comfortable view of a world divided between North and South and a morality which linked the prospects for development with the largesse of the North.

Three phenomena stand out today. The first is the spectacular success of the economies in East Asia. The second is the amazing transfer of wealth from the developing world back to the developed world which is one of the bizarre consequences of the severe indebtedness of the developing world, particularly Latin America. The third is the dismal cycle of famine and poverty in sub-Saharan Africa.

Two major changes have occurred. It is now accepted that

substantial increases of aid will not provide the solutions in the developing world, and the importance of encouraging markets is appreciated more widely. The target of raising aid levels in industrialized countries to 0.7 per cent of GDP was set and reset in the 1960s and 1970s. The Nordic countries and the Netherlands apart, the industrialized world did not meet these targets. But worse than this, the overall flow of capital from the developed to the developing world has reversed. Government aid has always been a small proportion of the capital supplied to developing countries. In the 1980s, because of the need to service the costs of debt in the Third World, the net movement of capital was from the capital starved Third World to the capital rich industrialized world. While overall growth in the developing world was on average higher than in the industrialized world, the kick start for self-sustaining growth was not there.

While the overall picture is not good there have been significant developments which have altered basic presumptions about where the responsibility for action to redress the situation lies. Some developing countries have grown so fast that they are now talked about as nearly developed. These are predominantly in East Asia – South Korea, Taiwan, Singapore and Hong Kong. They are countries which have chosen to develop export markets as one of the bases of growth; and have deliberately built industries that are internationally competitive.

These countries contrast sharply with those developing countries which opted for industrialization and import substitution, relying on aid to fund the start up and protection to get industry going. Others opted for centrally planned economic systems which also directed resources to developing greater self-sufficiency. Some adopted an indigenous version of socialism, others communist systems. Almost without exception these countries still depend on official aid at the end of the 1980s as much, if not more, than they did two decades before. Like their doctrinal mentors in Europe, those with centrally planned systems face major decisions about whether they can sustain the systems which they have created.

Interesting global contrasts now exist. Kenya is one of the more successful economies in Africa. It opted to allow a market economy to develop. Growth has been good over the past two decades. In contrast, Tanzania chose a heavily regulated socialist model. It has major problems of poverty, distribution, poor services and no end to dependence on aid. North and South Korea provide startling contrasts of high growth and prosperity and stagnation and debt. In South-east Asia there has been dramatic growth in the archipelagic ASEAN countries and stagnation in riparian Indo-China. Admittedly the latter has been locked in war. But in the major economy, Vietnam, it is recognized that market forces need to be released if there is to be growth.

Liberal economists have always been confident of the benefits of trade liberalization. Their economics told them that what worked in one economy would work in another. They argued that 'trade not aid' was the prescription. Trading and trade opportunities always offered much greater economic rewards for developing economies than aid.

New imperatives

In 1987 developing countries accounted for about 17 per cent of world trade – US$490 billion of a total of US$2,900 billion. It is instructive to examine which sectors of trade are subject to the highest incidence of protection and the respective levels of development among developing country exporters in these sectors (Figure 3.1).

The two largest components of exports from the developing countries are fuels (mainly petroleum products) and machinery and transport equipment. There are no major trade barriers of the conventional type applying to trade in fuels. Almost all of the exports of machinery and transport equipment are accounted for by exports from the Asian 'tigers' – Taiwan, Hong Kong, Singapore and South Korea. These countries face some significant barriers in the export of products in these categories. But compared to the majority of developing countries, their problems are mature.

If fuel and machinery exports are set aside the next two major categories of developing country trade are food and clothing and textiles. These are major categories of trade for a significant number of developing countries. Aside from the Asian tigers, clothing accounts for at least 20 per cent of the exports of

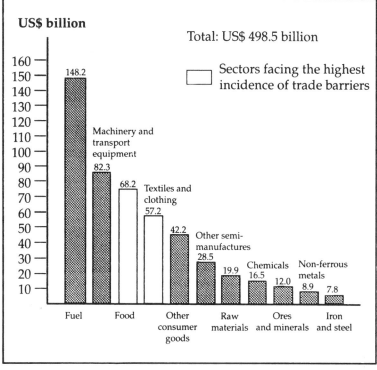

Source: GATT

FIGURE 3.1 *Exports from developing countries, 1987*

manufactures from 19 other developing countries. Of the 15 highly indebted countries food is the primary export item to industrialized countries for 9 of them.

Yet food and textiles and clothing are the two most heavily protected markets in the industrialized world. These are products which in the main developing countries produce more cheaply than industrialized countries. The international Multi-Fibre Arrangement (MFA), to which most industrialized countries belong, places detailed restrictions on the imports of clothing and textiles. But it only imposes restrictions on exports from developing countries. There are no restrictions on imports from other industrialized countries. Imports of food into the biggest markets, Europe, the United States and Japan, are heavily restricted. In comparison the markets in the industrialized world for machinery are relatively open.

There are no moral grounds upon which such obvious self-interest can be justified. It is not as if these were matters upon which universal national interest rested. In all the industrialized countries concerned there are interests arguing against the perpetuation of these high levels of protection. The real sin of this protection is not that it is a terrible waste of resources but that it is retarding significantly opportunities for growth in parts of the world where living standards are at levels which would be unacceptable in the industrialized world. This is a far greater moral imperative than a failure to be generous with aid.

Perverse generosity

The programmes to protect the agriculture and clothing and textile industries in the industrialized world are very expensive. They place high costs on the governments and also load a high cost on the consumer. In both sectors there are examples where some limited trade from selected developing country importers has been allowed. This access is usually held up as an example of generosity to demonstrate that protection is not damaging the interests of developing countries. However, the terms of this access can be fundamentally detrimental to the long-term interests of those countries.

These arrangements usually apply to poorer countries in the greatest need of foreign exchange. They are guaranteed the right to sell specified amounts of a product and are paid the high domestic price which the local protected manufacturer gets. For example, some small sugar growers in the Caribbean get paid at the same inflated level at which EC farmers, who cannot themselves compete at world prices, are paid.

In the short term this guaranteed access can create important economic benefits for small countries. Often in these cases, however, the country concerned would be better off with direct aid to encourage global competitiveness. Usually the small exporters with small guaranteed shares of highly protected markets remain tied to the high priced protected market.

If the market is closed or reduced the industry does not have an enduring value. There are a number of small Caribbean food and clothing producers who are tied to markets in the United States and the European Community on precisely these conditions. It is a misguided if not cynical form of generosity which encourages small countries with major development problems to develop industries which operate at the same level of inefficiency as protected industry in the industrialized world.

Global trade liberalization will not solve the economic problems of all developing countries, nor will it address all problems of development. These are often not simply economic problems. However, a concerted effort by industrialized countries to liberalize sectors of trade in which developing countries are efficient exporters as well as concomitant domestic liberalization by developing countries can, in the 1990s and beyond, stimulate growth, increase food production and help reduce the developing country debt burden.

Stimulating growth

The agriculture and apparel sectors are proven bases for growth in developing countries. In China and Thailand growth in agriculture stimulated growth in the rest of the economy. It is clear that such heavy protection as exists in global agricultural markets can depress prices in domestic markets. There are also numerous cases of local agricultural industries being left to collapse because cheaper products were available from heavily subsidized markets in the European Community or the United States.

Economists are divided about how various developing country exporters would benefit from liberalization of trade in textiles and clothing. Because existing arrangements have provided guaranteed levels of trade, it is generally assumed that if they are liberalized, the exporters which have benefited most from them – Taiwan, South Korea Hong Kong – would lose trade to other developing countries which are more efficient.

China, India, Pakistan and Bangladesh are likely to increase significantly exports of clothing if global arrangements are liberalized. It is interesting to note that it is in these countries that the bulk of the increase in the world's population by the end of the century will take place. It would be a major factor in creating successful development strategies if these countries were able to increase productivity in their economies to handle the additional population.

Feeding the world

Grain traders have a very clinical way of looking at the world. At the annual meeting of International Cereal Producers in Athens in September 1988, the manager in Geneva for Cargill, the world's largest trader of agricultural commodities, said the outlook for business for the end of the 1990s was good. First, the European Community, one of the largest, and most inaccessible, markets in the world, was likely to open up. This would result in more grain being traded (even within the Community). Second, the world 's population would increase by the end of the decade from 5 billion to 6.2 billion (See Figure 3.2). People had to be fed and production had to increase to achieve this.

The pattern of global food production defies the standard model beloved of those who like to divide the world cosily between what the rich do well – make cars and heavy machinery – and what the poor do well – grow coffee and weave materials. The United States and the European Community are among the largest agricultural producers and exporters in the world. They are not in this position for the right reasons, however.

Farmers in western Europe have been encouraged to produce because government authorities buy the produce at prices which are much higher than the farmers would get if they relied on prices obtainable on international markets. To protect these schemes, cheaper produce from other parts of the world is kept away from consumers in Europe. This also happens in the United States although the pattern of protection for some sectors is light and in almost all cases some cheaper imported produce is allowed into the country.

At the end of the 1970s and in the early 1980s we witnessed one of the most bizarre examples of how protecting business from market forces can turn the world on its head. While there was starvation in parts of Africa, the European Community was

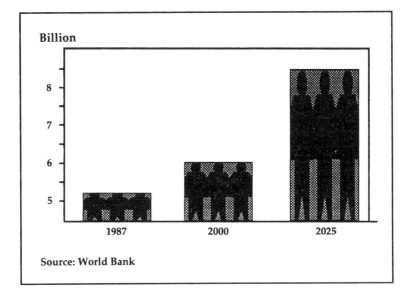

FIGURE 3.2 *World population growth*

spending between two and four billion dollars a year storing food that it could not consume or sell. Farmers in Belgium were able to sell their sugar to officials in Brussels for 35US cents a pound. The Community had to get rid of it so it unloaded a lot on the world market. The price plummeted, eventually falling to 5US cents. In some parts of the developing world, such as the Philippines, fragile regional economies collapsed as sugar farmers ceased production because the price was too low. In Japan consumers were paying US$50.00 a kilo for beef that was available in the United States or Australia for between US$10 and 15. Japanese shoppers were paying four times what Thai shoppers were paying for their rice.

In most industrialized countries governments have succumbed to political pressure from farmers to keep them in business. This might not have mattered if it did not affect the rest of the world – but it does. A number of factors affect agricultural production – bad handling, poor transport, overcropping and overgrazing. These are not trade problems and solving them is outside the direct capacity of governments in the industrialized world. A vital factor is making agricultural production efficient and sustainable. Trade barriers have a been a major hindrance. There is one very important aspect of production which is entirely within the capacity of the government of the Western World to address: that is the price the product can fetch.

Raising prices and importing

One of the keys to boosting agricultural production in the developing world is to raise prices. This may seem confusing. Why make food more expensive? The answer is to make farming worthwhile to farmers. If farmers can make a profit they will grow more. The Communist rulers in Eastern Europe discovered that this was one of the simpler ways of increasing food production. The World Bank has been prescribing this medicine for years. It has also been found in a number of countries that growth in the agricultural sector can trigger growth in the economy at large.

Two factors have traditionally depressed agricultural prices. The first is deliberate depression of the price of food by governments in developing countries – developing country growers can be required to sell to their own governments which pay low prices. Often the governments will even sell that food on at a loss, subsidizing the consumer. The second factor is heavy government subsidy of production by farmers in the industrialized world. They pay their farmers a high price for produce which is usually sold at a lower price to the consumers (reversing the process in developing countries) and the loss is paid for by taxes. This can depress the prices of export products available on the world market. The most direct effect occurs when these governments in industrialized countries unload their agricultural surpluses on the world markets for almost any price (since the produce has already been paid for). Purchase is then tempting for countries with food shortages facing demand they cannot satisfy. A few years ago a Peruvian government agency chose to buy surplus, subsidized dairy produce which was available from Europe because of overproduction. It was cheaper than the local product. As a result the local dairy industry declined.

One of the more appalling arguments used to support overproduction of agriculture in the industrialized world has been that at least it generates surpluses which can be used to supply cheap food to developing countries. Some net food importers have benefited. But far more developing countries have been penalized because of the reduction of domestic prices and productivity. The United States used to make cheap wheat available under a food assistance program called PL480. It was cheap and available from surplus production. India took grain under this programme for years. When India decided to stimulate domestic wheat production, one of the actions critical to success was to cease taking the cheaper US wheat. Productivity in its grain sector improved eventually enabling India to cease importing wheat altogether.

It is not enough that the United States and the European Community cease overproducing and dumping the excess on the world market and in the process depressing prices and returns for farmers in other countries. In large markets they do affect other economies.

The industrialized countries have an obligation to open their markets to imports from developing countries, at world market prices; indeed, they have the obligation to do so but to all countries. This is one of the fundamental tenets of GATT membership. Industrialized countries insist that others join the GATT and open up their markets – usually to manufactured goods from the industrialized world.

Trading out of debt

For many countries in the developing world the 1980s were a 'lost decade'. The debt burden has crippled development programmes and for some countries growth has stagnated or reversed and standards of living have fallen. Between 1980 and 1987 per capita consumption among the 17 most heavily indebted countries is estimated to have fallen 1.6 per cent. The cost of paying for the debt has become crippling. Capital is now flowing from the developing world to the industrialized world. Whereas in 1981 net capital inflows to developing countries were about US$30 billion, developing countries as a group are now paying about US$30 billion per year more to the rich countries than they are receiving in loans.

Several actions need to be taken simultaneously to handle the debt problem.

1. Restoration of capital flows.
2. Internal economic reform to reduce government costs, liberalize economies, raise savings and increase competitiveness.
3. Debt re-structuring and debt write off.
4. Lower interest rates.
5. Better trading opportunities.

None of these actions is easy and they require coordinated action across a range of international bodies. There is a significant contribution to be made through global trade liberalization in the Uruguay Round negotiations. Increasing the export markets for products from indebted countries would generate the income upon which growth could be based. It would reduce the percentage of export earnings that has to be earmarked to pay interest on debt (this was up to 35 per cent for the heavily indebted developing countries in 1987). Food is the primary export item to industrialized countries for nine of fifteen countries identified by the IMF as 'most heavily indebted' (see Table 3.1).

There are some very stark relationships between constraints to trade and capacity to pay back debt. In 1986 economists for the World Bank estimated that if international markets for meat were liberalized globally Argentina's foreign exchange earnings would increase by US$3.2 billion. This is greater than the interest Argentina pays on its external debt.

Increases in export receipts would also enable these countries to import more. Between 1980 and 1987 they cut imports at an annual rate of 6.3 per cent. This probably increased the US trade deficit by US$15–20 billion in the early 1980s. Agreement to liberalize markets would be a key contribution to global efforts to bring the developing country debt problem under control.

TABLE 3.1 *Most heavily indebted developing countries*

Country	US$ billions	%/GDP	Debt service %/exports
Brazil*	106.1	33.7	33.2
Mexico	96.9	69.6	38.4
Argentina*	50.3	65.5	52.0
Venezuela	32.7	67.8	32.4
Nigeria	26.1	111.3	11.7
Philippines*	23.8	69.4	25.7
Yugoslavia	19.5	32.2	19.4
Morocco*	18.8	117.9	30.8
Chile*	18.0	103.6	26.4
Colombia*	15.4	45.3	36.3
Peru	13.9	31.2	12.9
Côte d'Ivoire*	11.7	124.1	40.8
Ecuador*	9.1	93.2	21.9
Bolivia	4.8	115.6	22.1
Uruguay*	3.2	44.2	25.7

Source: *1989 World Development Report*, GATT
* Where food is the primary export item to industrialized countries

A collaborative effort

To secure the full benefit of liberalization by industrialized countries developing countries should liberalize their own economies as well. This works at a variety of levels but one simple aspect is competitiveness. To sell into a global market it is necessary to produce at the level of global competitiveness. If a heavily protected market is opened but a potential exporter is not positioned to sell into the market or has not increased domestic efficiency, the full benefit of new markets cannot be secured.

The OECD has calculated that liberalization of trade in agriculture will yield a benefit to the OECD countries of US$45 billion. If developing countries liberalize at the same time their economies will benefit by a total of US$18 billion. But if the developing countries do not liberalize they will have a net loss to their economies of US$12 billion.

Similarly with the textiles industries, unless developing countries liberalize their own industries to ensure that they are operating at the most efficient level possible, they will not be in a position to exploit the opportunities which would arise from the opening of markets in the industrialized world.

Most developing countries still argue that it is more difficult for them to liberalize than for developed countries. In GATT a principle of 'special and differential treatment for developing countries' (known in GATT shorthand as 'S and D') is invoked. Where new obligations for liberalization are agreed the principle is asserted that the burden of obligation should be lighter for developing countries.

There is a vigorous debate about whether or not the rules of economics apply differently in developing countries. The vast majority of developing countries contend that there is a difference. A number of the more successful developing countries now express private scepticism. Putting aside the issue of whether or not any qualitative difference does exist there is a virtual consensus that, in general, developing countries need more time than industrialized countries to phase in cutbacks in protection.

A development opportunity

Trade liberalization will not address all development problems. But of all the options available to the industrialized world to address development problems over the next decade, it is the one within reach which can have the most dramatic effect. Protection of inefficient industry in the industrialized world, particularly in the agricultural and clothing and textiles sectors, has suppressed opportunities for growth in the developing world. Liberalization of these markets would increase exports from a significant number of developing countries.

The remarkable thing about this is that if the Europeans, North Americans and Japanese liberalized, they would enjoy very significant economic gains. The OECD has estimated that in the industrialized world the total subsidy paid to farmers by tax payers and consumers is around US$200 billion per year. One recent American estimate is that complete liberalization of apparel and textiles in the United States would generate an annual gain to consumers of US$20 billion.

The Uruguay Round is a very significant opportunity for countries to commit themselves to global programmes of trade liberalization which can improve opportunities for growth in a number of developing countries, help to ease the developing country debt burden and increase global food production.

Chapter Four

THE TRADE CHALLENGES OF THE 1990s –
efficiency and growth

Who wants to compete?

In the best selling 'Iacocca An Autobiography' (Bantam 1984), Lee Iacocca compared the condition of the Chrysler Motor Company when he first joined it in 1978 with Ford which he had just left:

> The Ford Motor Company had become a disaster because the old man ran it so poorly. He knew nothing about sound business practices. In those days, companies were routinely run by swashbuckling entrepreneurs rather than planners and managers.
>   But Chrysler was even worse. Chrysler couldn't blame its condition on its founder, who came from another era. The Chrysler fiasco had occurred after thirty years of scientific management. That in 1978 a huge company should be still run like a small grocery store was incomprehensible.

Any expectation that Iacocca's own sound business practices might be based on free trade principles and a willingness to compete with the best of them on the international stage is dashed when Iacocca addresses the 'Japanese challenge' towards the end of the book. Iacocca writes:

> We have to take action. We must replace free trade with fair trade. If Japan – or any other nation – protects its markets,

we should be doing the same. If they encourage local industry, we should respond in kind. And if they play tricky games with their currency, we should take steps to equalize the exchange rate.'

Contrast this with this extract from the postscript of *Xerox American Samurai – The Behind the Scenes Story of How A Corporate Giant Beat the Japanese at Their Own Game* (Jacobson and Hillkirk, Collier 1986):

> If there's one certainty about the copier industry – and all of American industry – it's that the business of doing business is not going to get any easier, especially in manufacturing. The easy way out would be for American companies to shift all of their production offshore, to the least costly venue, or for the American government to institute protectionist barriers. Those, however are only short term solutions. They are an admission that American companies can't be competitive and never will be competitive. Over the long haul, such measures endanger the American economy as well as the world's. Xerox has determined that to be a world-class company, to reach its goal of $30 billion to $35 billion in sales by 1992, it has to be a strong manufacturing and design company everywhere it operates in the world. It has to be competitive everywhere.

This answer would have been the prevailing view in corporate America in the late 1960s. In the early 1970s, the Japanese launched into global markets for automobiles, TV sets, video recorders and miniaturized electronics. They were sensationally successful. The popular parlour game in board rooms in the United States and Europe was to wonder why this had happened, why they could not compete. There were lots of easy, comforting answers – Japanese wages were lower; the work ethic was different; Japanese women workers had nimbler fingers and were more adept at assembling miniaturized electronics; and Japanese marketing practices were predatory. Iacocca had plenty of company in Europe. Board members of the Dutch giant Philips regularly argued the need for protection against the Japanese.

The most potent complaint against the Japanese was that they did not trade fairly because they did not import. There is a valid point here. Japan's share of import of manufactures is well below that of the other major traders. Imports are beginning to increase but the rate of change is gradual. Nevertheless, wiser heads knew that there was a much more difficult and worrying issue which had nothing to do with Japan's import performance – the Japanese were simply producing more efficiently. This was a much harder issue to deal with.

The Japanese onslaught was halted with a variety of protectionist measures, most of which disregarded GATT principles for international competitiveness. The Italians would not allow more than 3,000 Japanese cars a year to be imported. About the only time Italians saw Japanese motor cycles was as they monotonously took line honours in Grand Prix races. For six months in the early 1980s, the French throttled the flow of imports of Japanese video recorders into France by requiring them to pass through a small customs inspection post at Poitiers in central France. The United States 'encouraged' the Japanese to comply with orderly marketing arrangements and to impose 'voluntary' restraint arrangements under which imports were held to agreed or understood levels.

The basic issue here for international business is not whether some arcane GATT rules are respected or broken; it is whether or not companies consider that it is in their own best interests to compete and make profits at the most competitive standard.

Efficiency and/or profit

Most people in business learn early that growth in profits is not automatically synonymous with commitment to free market principles. This is especially true in sectors where products are traded. There are some very rich textile and clothing manufacturers around the world who owe their wealth to government measures which protect their businesses from more efficient competition. Import licences can also be wonderful ways to make money. The most valuable one is that which grants an exclusive right to import a product which has no direct competitor. The importer is in a strong position to charge as high a price as possible for the product without having to worry about being undercut by a cheaper product.

If protection of profits is the objective the device used may not matter. There is not a lot of difference between a monopoly right to import motor vehicles – which is common in developing countries – and the imposition of quotas like those France and Italy have used to control imports of motor cars from Japan. The basic problem is that the industry being protected never becomes efficient. Protection of the US motor industry is a very good case in point.

Alarm at the increased share of the US market won by the Japanese automobile exporters led US manufacturers in the early 1980s to seek protection from the US government. Following precedents from the steel and consumer electronics industries Japanese exporters were encouraged to limit the number of cars they exported to the United States. As a result Japan's share of the US car market fell 3 per cent over four years. But the US consumer still wanted Japanese cars and the Japanese car makers increased their profit margins. The dollar price of Japanese cars rose 42 per cent in the same period. Before restrictions were imposed the list price in the United States was 9 per cent higher than the list price in Japan for the comparable car. Four years later US prices were 35 per cent higher.

It is interesting to examine how the Japanese industry handled this situation. Much of the profit was ploughed into programmes for research and development and increasing productivity. The Japanese product became even more competitive than the American product. While some reinvestment took place in the US industry US producers remained insulated from competitive pressures and were not significantly better able to compete. By the late 1980s the Japanese restraints had become truly voluntary. The US motor industry still did not believe that it could compete without them. Modernization of production in the US motor industry does appear to be taking place: but less from the breathing space which protection from the Japanese imports was supposed to create than from construction by the Japanese motor vehicle manufacturing plants in the United States.

This is a happier story than some. In other areas of trade not all exporters have the wit to plough their windfall profits into research to increase productivity. Some allow their own costs of production to drift towards the level of costs of the more expensive product that is being shielded from them. In time they drift towards the level of non-competitiveness of the product which they originally set out to undercut.

If over time the market for an imported product is cut back, the formerly efficient exporter may even go out of business if this is a major market. This more extreme effect has been seen with agricultural exporters. This is the risk facing manufacturing plants set up by US, Taiwanese, Hong Kong or Korean capital in small Caribbean or Indian Ocean countries with the purpose of supplying specialist clothing markets which have been opened up in the US apparel market which can be quickly closed following pressure from domestic producers.

Maintaining competitiveness

Vigorous global growth in the 1990s and beyond will require active competition in global markets. Maintaining efficiency in big business will be one of the major challenges. There are trends which can beguile international business into operating at levels of suboptimal efficiency. Global companies are necessary to compete in international markets but formation of global conglomerates exposes companies to the risk of the lethargy of hugeness. Fear of competition and the cost of research into high technology encourages global strategic alliances. But these can pit profit against efficiency. And any drift towards trade blocs carries dangers. The temptation for business would be to settle into that sphere and become insulated from the competitive stimulus of global competition.

There are two global trends which have emerged in the 1980s and which offer significant opportunities for business. The first is a global trend to liberalize economies to give greater scope to market forces. The second is the internationalization of markets and the internationalization of trade in services. The maximum benefit of these opportunities for business will only be achieved it there is a functioning, global, open trade system.

Both are threatened by protectionism and inclinations to regional trade arrangements in Europe and North America.

Regional economic arrangements in themselves are no problem. But when they operate to reduce exposure to international markets and reduce competitiveness, opportunities for growth are reduced and efforts by business to set up global scale operations are threatened.

The market resplendent

The 1980s will be remembered as the era of the market resplendent. The politics of Reaganism and Thatcherism set the tone for the decade. The emphasis among industrial countries has been on deregulation and privatization. There is a paradox here since the early part of the decade witnessed an upsurge of protectionism in the United States and no diminution of protection in the European Community against competitive products from Japan and East Asia. The focus on the upsurge of protectionism has tended to obscure the parallel interest in liberalization.

Significant programmes of unilateral liberalization have been introduced in a number of countries. Developing countries which have liberalized or have begun programmes include Chile, Mexico, Turkey, Taiwan, Korea, Kenya, Costa Rica, Panama, Indonesia, and Malaysia. Argentina and Brazil are using liberalization as part of strategies to defeat inflation. Australia and New Zealand have acted strongly to reduce the protection in their manufacturing sectors, which was the highest in the industrialized world.

All Eastern European countries have now embarked on programmes to convert their economies to market economies. In the European Community the programme to create a single market will have a liberalizing effect on the economies of the member states and engender a stronger sense of competition in some sectors of business. There is also an appreciation in Europe and the United States that it is time to consider reform of the heavily protected agricultural sectors and to institutionalize international deregulation of the services sectors. In Japan there is acceptance that there has to be greater liberalization of the economy, even if this is in response to intense international pressure from the United States and to a lesser extent from the European Community.

Chip-led growth and global markets

It can take four seconds for a purchase in Singapore made on a credit card account held in Quebec to be finalized, with all the accounts cleared and the payments made. These are services transactions that support an export and an import. The services themselves are exported and imported as well. And transactions made with this speed and efficiency themselves stimulate growth. These transactions could not have happened without the development of information technology and the revolution it is causing in communications. The capacity to trade services quickly and efficiently will be one of the basic requirements for global economic growth in the next half century.

Capital now moves around the world at dizzying speed. It has become one of the human activities that is truly international. The nationality of a loan facility is impossible to establish if it has been put together by a collection of banks drawing on funds in different markets around the world. Capital markets have been created which do not respect any national or supranational authority. The money is permanently off shore.

'Global Markets' are now bywords in business strategy. Global operation is not new. American multinationals such as IBM have been operating globally for decades. European multinationals have been active in the United States for a long time. BP is now the 18th largest company in the United States. What is new is that markets around the world are no longer segmented.

Capital is a globally priced commodity. A supplier of one large regional market cannot afford for long to pay for capital at a price much higher than a competitor supplying into an adjacent market. For high technology products the cost of development of new products can be so high that sometimes it can only be managed comfortably if the market for which the product is planned is a global market. Market intelligence is now deeper, more quickly gathered and updated, available in 'real time' and more readily digestible than ever before.

Global markets need to be serviced on a global scale, and that means efficiently. This is probably the fundamental importance of efforts to start to liberalize trade in services. It is essential to building the basis for growth over the next two decades.

'Trading' services?

For many businesses in the services sector, the idea that they are 'trading' is novel. Tariffs and quotas are obvious barriers to trade. They raise the price of the imported product above the selling price in its country of origin. Bankers are only starting to realize that regulations which restrict what services a foreign owned bank might offer or how they might be offered as compared to a domestic bank are restrictions to their ability to trade their products.

A regulation which sets technical standards which prevent a foreign telecommunications company connecting to a domestic network is also a barrier to trade. (The effect of this – a means of restricting imports – is probably too well appreciated by national telecommunications authorities.) Banks and finance companies need regularly to transfer electronically vast amounts of data. Regulations requiring these transfers to be made through a government owned telecommunications facility restrict trade, regardless of whether other means are available.

Bankers, insurance executives, construction engineers, telecommunications engineers and transport company executives are today being challenged to look at what they do in a different light when they operate internationally.

One of the characteristics of service industries is that they have become accustomed to operating in a regulated environment. Governments set prudential requirements for banks and insurance companies. Governments have allocated broadcast bands for telecommunications broadcasters. 'The post' was regarded in the nineteenth century as such a sacred trust that only government could be trusted to do it – and in most countries the telegraph was regarded as an electronic version of the post.

In the services sector creating international operations has tended to be viewed by executives in those businesses as a process of linking existing businesses operating within national regulatory frameworks. There has been no choice. The most outstanding example is how telecommunications companies did this. They agreed to 'connect' their services, with each carrying the message originating from the other's system to its destination in the home carrier's system.

Costs were shared by a formula which was negotiated and

took no account of relative costs of operation in each carrier. As a result, if one of the carriers is efficient and low cost, and as a result attracts more business than the other carrier, the efficient carrier cannot offer the full benefits of its better prices even to the nationals using its system since it has to pay part of its less efficient partner's costs. The economic option – to be able to competitively offer the more efficient service into the market – is not available.

The concept of applying the principles of international trade to services revolutionizes thinking and fundamentally expands the established idea of trade. This is a critical development. Not only will global growth be influenced by providing a basis for expansion of trade in services. The ability to trade services efficiently is also becoming one of the critical components which determine how goods can be traded efficiently. It affects how quickly finance can be organized, how quickly orders can be processed, how quickly market information can be gathered, processed and absorbed, and how the cost of the services input into the manufacturing process can be cut.

A new trend

Services themselves are becoming an increasingly important component of world trade. In 1987 global exports of services were nearly 20 per cent of world trade. This makes them equal to exports of food and fuels, or to motor vehicles and electronics. GATT's statistics show that services trade has grown more rapidly than traditional trade in goods in the eighties (see Figure 4.1).

To create a picture of the global breakdown of world trade in services GATT's economists have identified three general categories:

1. Transport (goods and people) – 30 per cent of global services trade.
2. Tourist expenditure (at destination) – 30 per cent.
3. Private services and income (labour income, telecommunications, financial services) – 40 per cent.

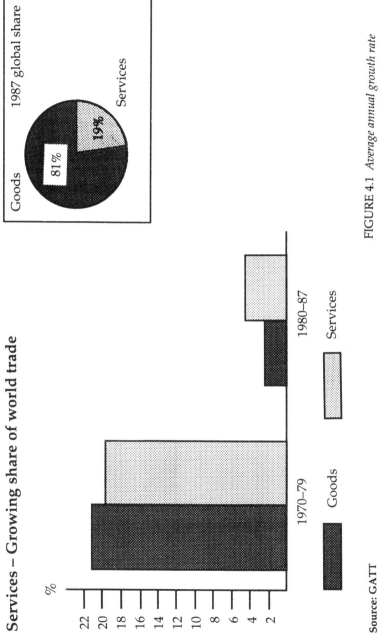

Services – Growing share of world trade

FIGURE 4.1 *Average annual growth rate*

Source: GATT

The trade is probably bigger than these figures suggest. The full extent of trade in services is not known because many governments do not yet collect statistics on exports and imports of services. Existing statistics do not record trans-border flows of electronic data which is one of the most rapidly growing sectors of services trade. The GATT points out that spending in the United States on information technology hardware and software has risen in 1970 from $24 billion to $360 billion in 1985. Most of this stock is owned by the service sectors, half of it by the communications sector.

The new efficiencies

By the end of the 1990s, the services industries themselves will account for a much larger share of global trade. This is as certain as the continuing growth of information technology which is one of the driving forces of services expansion. One of the keys to stimulating global growth in the 1990s and beyond will be promoting efficiency in international trade in the services industries. Technology may be our most important helpmate. Already it is demonstrating that business will simply flow around regulatory impediments. For many international financial transactions there is no practical concept of nationality.

It will be of critical importance to create a framework in which the competitive principles of price and efficiency are encouraged to exert maximum impact on international trade in services. In this respect, regulation will be the enemy. It is vital that there is agreement in the Uruguay Round negotiations on an agreement on services that lays out international rules for applying multilateral principles for a liberal trading system.

The importance of the services negotiations has been under-rated. An enormous boost to global growth would be achieved by commitments by the European Community and the United States to phase out the various protective arrangements and non-tariff arrangements that weaken the multilateral trading system and hinder trade in manufactures. Basic commitments to this are needed. In the longer run, however, it may be that a framework for future liberalization of international services will be more important for boosting growth in the industrialized economies.

Epilogue to Part I

The political and economic order of Europe is under reconstruction. The Eastern European countries are turning to GATT to help introduce market economies. The European Community is poised to advance European integration dramatically. Developing countries are liberalizing. The Pacific century is approaching and information technology is altering the face of international trade. There is no better time to reflect on the role of a system of international rules to encourage global, open trade; and to act to make it serve the needs of the next decade and century.

If we gaze into the crystal ball, we can see some possibilities which show how different that world will be in 2000 in comparison to the one that existed in 1950 and was the crucible in which the GATT was forged:

1. Two global engines of growth – trans-Pacific and pan-European.
2. Germany the unambiguous leader of Europe, the trans-Atlantic axis of leadership being Berlin–Washington.
3. Acceptance as commonplace of a transcontinental concept of Europe as a political and economic entity, in which German will be the second lingua franca after English.
4. A European Community of 16 (including Norway, Sweden, Hungary and Austria).

5. The Community will be struggling with inadequate and expensive programmes to develop Poland, Yugoslavia, Romania and the Soviet Confederation.

6. The Confucian ethic will rival the Protestant ethic as the human system of values regarded as most nurturing growth and prosperity.

7. Trans-Pacific economic relations will be well developed and there will be a PACED – Pacific Organization for Economic Cooperation and Development.

8. The Japanese economy will be more open and the US/ Japanese relationship will be more equal than at present.

9. The dragons and tigers in the Pacific region will collectively equal a powerful global trade group and will mitigate the preponderance of Japanese economic power.

10. China will experiencing another burst of growth to match that of the early 1980s and Hong Kong will be the centre of this boom.

11. There will be vibrant economic growth in the Western hemisphere – Mexico will enjoy some form of preferential trade relationship with the United States (and thereby, through the free trade agreement, with Canada) – and Chile will be a leading economy.

These things may not happen as described; but the forces which allow them to be postulated now will cause outcomes related to these possibilities. These are the forces which will shape the global order and which international arrangements governing trade will have to capture and satisfy. In 1982 when Bill Brock, as the then US special trade representative, began to advocate another multilateral trade round, some of the most important developments which global trade liberalization now needs to satisfy were not apparent.

The Uruguay Round has the luck that any enterprise of this type needs to succeed. It is probable that if the Round had not been launched before the European Community's single market programme got under way or the revolution in Eastern Europe had occurred it would have been stillborn. The Tokyo Round, the previous set of international trade negotiations, did not have luck. It started in 1973 and did not conclude until 1979. Most of the work was done in a concentrated burst over the last eighteen months. The attention of participating governments was sidetracked by the two oil price hikes and the effort to structure international economic relations in response. Industrial countries were also grappling with the problems of stagflation and developing countries were staggering under the burden of major balances of payments problems. There are also very substantial differences between then and now, the most important being the much more ambitious agenda for the Uruguay Round.

One of the remarkable aspects of the Uruguay Round is that it has not been turned off course by the revitalisation of the European Community through the Single Market programme or the collapse of the Soviet order in Eastern Europe, two of the most significant events of the last quarter of the twentieth century. On the contrary, the Round has enjoyed the relatively concentrated attention of governments. Global growth has been steady and this has created the most benign environment in which to contemplate trade liberalization. There has been a confluence of leaders in the major economies who wish to liberalize and restore the credibility of the GATT system and there is something approaching a confluence of interests among the major participants who all want something out of the Round.

In April 1989 the Jamaican ambassador to GATT until 1989, Tony Hill, told the Trade Negotiations Committee (the steering body for the Uruguay Round), that in his opinion the Uruguay Round was 'doomed to succeed'. The omens are right. The danger is that governments may let the opportunity slip through their fingers.

Part Two

THE PLAYERS

Chapter Five
YEUTTER'S ROUND –
the United States

Clayton Yeutter was unusually qualified to serve as the US Trade Representative (USTR), which he did between 1985 and 1988. He was chairman of the Chicago Mercantile Exchange when approached by the Reagan administration after the 1984 presidential election to serve as USTR. He was invariably polite but also straight to the point. He had done a stint a few years earlier as a deputy USTR and was familiar with how GATT worked and how it did not work. He personally believed in the multilateral trading system.

Getting the Uruguay Round launched was one of the bits of undone business in the files handed over by his predecessor, Bill Brock. Ever since the failed meeting of GATT ministers in 1982 the United States had been canvassing the idea of a new Round of international trade negotiations.

Yeutter not only inherited an elegant office in the restored Civil War building that housed the office of the USTR, he inherited one of the characters of international trade – Michael B. Smith. Smith had worked for three previous USTR's as deputy, including a stint as the US ambassador to the GATT. He had also been a textile negotiator which is regarded as a badge of honour among former textile negotiators; but they are noted by others for bad habits – like believing that the only time to begin negotiating is after the deadline has expired and an entirely sleepless night.

Despite his State Department background, Smith was

well-known for his undiplomatic demeanour, in which he revelled. He would don a brightly coloured baseball cap with his otherwise standard Washington buttondown shirt and pinstripe suit when negotiations were getting pointless or nowhere.

Yeutter faced a difficult time as USTR. Pressure had been mounting in Congress for tough unilateral trade measures the like of which had not been seen in thirty years. The US current account had swung to a deficit of US$107 billion in 1984 from a surplus of US$2 billion in 1980. The country was gripped in a fever of soul searching about why the United States was no longer the major economic power and the grassroots politicians in Congress wanted action. They wanted to turn the deficit around by blocking imports, especially Japanese imports. This would have fatally crippled the international trading system set up in 1948.

The solution to the trade deficit was to be found in macroeconomic, not trade, policy. The US dollar was too high and the country was on a spending binge. The proper means of dealing with these problems required challenges to the orthodoxies of Reaganomics, not artificial management of trade. But no one of influence seemed able or prepared to tackle the basic problem – cutting the budget deficit: it was bad politics.

Clayton Yeutter's strategy was to get the Uruguay Round under way to channel pressures for protectionism into multilateral negotiations; negotiate the best possible trade bill by keeping to a minimum the levers for bilateral trade pressure that Congress wanted in the bill; and to keep attention focused on the possibility that the United States might negotiate free trade agreements if there was no support for launching a multilateral trade negotiation. He stuck to this and it worked.

Yeutter was personally committed to seeing a trade round launched and to seeing that it included as priority items liberalization of agriculture and services. It was also his idea that there should be a mid term review of the Round and that interim results should be negotiated. He set the objectives and his staff delivered. The Uruguay Round is Yeutter's Round.

The special role of the United States

The cynic may observe, not without accuracy, that the United States and Great Britain were both advocates of free trade in the nineteenth and twentieth centuries while both were the dominant international traders or while their industries were the most efficient compared to their international competitors. Nevertheless, it has been the United States which has most persistently argued for reductions of international barriers to trade since GATT was founded and which has been the driving force behind nearly every round of trade negotiations.

Until the mid-1970s, the driving force behind the adoption of these positions by the US administration was US manufacturing. However, since that time US manufacturing has faded from the scene as a force for liberal trade. Major companies have switched sides and become the new forces for protection in the United States.

With the election of the Reagan administration, however, a strong ideological commitment to free trade remained. And as the US trade deficit rose so did the Congressional inclination to be protectionist. The administration saw it as in its interest to have an international trade negotiation initiated. This would channel Congressional energies into a framework where other international considerations would have to be taken into account. It would forestall arguments for adoption in Congress of measures which would clearly damage US economic interests and cause the United States major international difficulties.

Since the early 1980s a new US interest group favouring free trade had gradually emerged. It has been driven by Jim Robinson of American Express and John Reed of Citibank. Both corporations had started to feel frustrated at their inability to do business easily in other countries. They picked up on the idea that the GATT concepts of international rules to govern trade, with adjudicative processes to deal with complaints that the rules were not being respected, were concepts that could be extended to trade in services.

They were not the first in this field. The British were. Since the late 1960s, a small lobby group called LOTIS had operated in the City. It was set up by William Clarke who is now Chairman of the merchant bank ANZ McCaughan. Its purpose was to try to get people to understand and government to accept that services were traded; and in the particular case of the United Kingdom, alarm about deficits in Britain's balance of trade would be reduced if the effect of Britain's nearly always favourable balance of trade in services were taken into account.

The administration found it both necessary and expedient to respond to the interests of this new lobby for liberal trade. It could not be ignored. It was also an important ally to the liberal trade advocates in the administration who needed the counter-vailing weight of this group to fend off protectionists in Congress. As pressures started to mount in Congress in the early 1980s, the US administration started to advocate more strongly the launching of a new international round of multi-lateral trade negotiations. Increasingly the United States was also arguing that this round had to include trade in services.

In the early 1980s the United States also started to raise doubts about its commitment to the multilateral trading system. These were different from the doubts about its commitment to multilateral trade which it generated from the mid-1970s by using various bilateral arrangements to stem excessively com-petitive imports.

The United States started to advertise the possibility of entering into its own free trade arrangements if other countries were not interested in a multilateral effort to revitalize the GATT system. Much of the impetus for this stemmed from one of the most disastrous events in the history of the GATT, known in shorthand as the 1982 GATT ministerial.

The Tokyo Round of multilateral trade negotiations was finally wound up in 1979. It began in 1973. It was supposed to last only two years. After fits and starts and long periods of inactivity it concluded with modest achievements. As the Tokyo Round was drawing to a close, resort by the United States and the European Community to special trade arrangements outside GATT for the most troublesome products intensified. This reflected the difficulty experienced by American and European administrations in handling the recession of the early 1980s. The consequence was that more and more trade was being locked into arrangements that conflicted with the GATT trading system and undermined it.

In 1981 a proposal emerged that trade ministers should meet

in GATT to renew the commitment to the GATT system of multilateral trade rules. GATT was unusual compared to most other international institutions in that there was no regular provision for ministers to meet. The only occasions when ministers did meet in GATT was to launch a series of formal international trade negotiations (like the meeting at Punta). They had only done so seven times in thirty years.

The idea of the 1982 ministerial turned out in hindsight to be a ghastly mistake. First, the meeting was convened at the nadir of a recession. Trade liberalization means restructuring of industry. Governments cannot contemplate new commitments to reduce protection when they are facing the pressures of recession – rising unemployment, demands to help failing industries, reduced income, higher social security costs. There is always a degree of involuntary restructuring during a recession when companies go broke. But governments can usually handle the domestic pressures that invariably arise when they accept obligations to reduce protection only when they have room to manoeuvre politically and room in the budget to meet some of the costs of restructuring.

Second, as preparations for this meeting proceeded, officials got more and more ambitious about what they would try to persuade ministers to agree on. By the time the meeting was convened officials had prepared an impossible set of proposals over which there were fundamental disagreements. It was clearly impossible for ministers to settle these issues in the time available. Ministers and officials belong to the same governments. If officials cannot settle disagreements, it is because there is a policy which it is not in their power to change. While a handful of key issues can be left to ministers if too much is left then it is simply impossible for ministers to settle things.

This is what happened at the 1982 GATT ministerial meeting. It was a failure and should not have been convened. This was probably the nadir of the GATT. At the time when the major traders were deliberately shifting significant proportions of world trade out of the GATT framework, a major GATT conference organized to address these problems comprehensively failed to do so. One byproduct was the beginning of dalliance in the United States, including in the administration, with the idea of building a network of free trade agreements with individual countries or groups of countries as an alternative to the GATT system.

The administration exploited this idea well. It was never clear whether the United States was using this as a threat to stampede other countries to the negotiating table to initiate a new trade round or whether it was a serious alternative. It was probably both. The free trade area approach yielded some results. An agreement was negotiated with Israel and another, much more important, with Canada. The fact was that it was the Canadian government which pressed for their agreement.

Once the Uruguay Round was running, first Clayton Yeutter and then his successor, Carla Hills, made firm statements that the alternative approach was dead. The United States would concentrate all its efforts on making a success of the Uruguay Round. In a very basic sense the Uruguay Round is the United States's Round. It proposed it, it lobbied for it, it got brand new issues, including services, on the agenda and continuously drove the process. If the United States had not done these things, there would not have been a trade round.

301 – curse and carrot

If there were numerology in international trade the numbers 301 would be especially ominous. This is the provision of the US Trade Act which empowers the administration to impose trade barriers on countries which do not measure up to criteria set in US law. The same Act provides the administration with the authority to negotiate multilaterally to reduce barriers and to reinforce the GATT system.

The United States is in the anomalous position of providing leadership to strengthen the multilateral trading system while at the same time adopting positions which imperil it.

'Don't move or I'll blow my brains out'

There have always been exceptions in practice to the general policy of successive US administrations of supporting the GATT multilateral trading system. Without wanting to encourage this, it can be said that this is relatively normal in international life. In a system which depends for its functioning on the voluntary surrender by governments of responsibilities to international jurisdiction, there is a need to provide for exceptions. It is surprising how many parties to GATT have them. But there is a qualitative difference with existing provisions in US trade law.

The Trade Act gives the administration an independent capacity first to judge how other countries trade against criteria which are set out in the Act and then to take unilateral action to redress situations which do not meet those criteria. These provisions are not an exception to the international legal commitments which the United States has entered into by acceding to GATT; they fundamentally contradict them.

As a party to GATT the United States accepts international trade laws, which specify the grounds upon which trade may be restricted. Other parties accept those laws as well. If a country breaks one of these laws there are established rights of redress and rules about what corrective action can be taken if a complaint that a rule has been broken is upheld.

More importantly, GATT supports liberal or free competition (or free trade) principles. Its laws commit parties to act only in ways that reinforce those principles. These principles determine the trade rules (for example that tariffs should be the instrument of trade protection) and redress (for example, if a country has to re-open a market after illegally closing it, it can only open it according to the GATT rule that all other parties to GATT get equal access to that market).

Under the US Trade Act the US administration can impose barriers on the imports of products from other GATT members on grounds that do not exist in the GATT. These grounds include an unacceptable human rights record, unacceptable labour standards, or 'unfair' trade practices. In isolation, these may not be unreasonable or unfounded concerns. But making provision in domestic law to link such provisions to extension or denial of access to markets does extraordinary damage to US efforts to strengthen multilateral principles of liberal and free trade. There are two principal effects.

The first is the thief effect. It is difficult to discourage someone else from being a thief if they see you stealing. It is worse if you are the leader of the scout troop. The United States has been the leader of the GATT scout troop since its inception. The second effect is to force countries to move some of their trade out of the GATT trade system. This is what happens if the United States imposes or raises a tariff on an import from a particular country because that country has not met a test which is not required under GATT but is provided for in US trade law. The free trade principle of the GATT is that everybody has the right to trade with everybody else on the same terms. This is the principle that rewards the most efficient producer.

All countries benefit from having access to the cheapest imports and being able to sell their products in the most open markets. The larger the country is as a trader, the greater is the benefit of access to the markets of others. For the United States to adopt policies that cause countries to remove trade from the GATT liberal trading system and denies its own citizens the opportunity to buy that product at the cheapest price is tantamount to holding a gun to its own head and threatening to shoot if its trading partner does not cooperate.

Dirty Harry

Some very significant liberalizations of markets, or promises to open markets, have taken place since the Uruguay Round began. Barriers to markets have been declared illegal through the GATT dispute settlement processes. Japan's decision in 1988 to open its beef market is one of the largest single acts of trade liberalization that has occurred in two decades. When fully open it will allow for US$2 billion more in imports. This decision was a courageous one by the Japanese government. It cost the Liberal Democrat Party significant electoral support.

In some respects this is one of the most significant effects to date of the Uruguay Round. Japan was pressed through the GATT's dispute procedures by the United States, Australia and New Zealand to open its market. However, it is not likely that Japan would have responded as it did without the international environment for trade liberalization which the Uruguay Round has created.

The United States, Australia and New Zealand also successfully challenged a complete ban on beef imports which Korea imposed in 1984. Korea has re-opened its beef market – by 1992 its annual beef imports will rise to 60,000 tonnes – and it has committed itself to opening the market further. The European Community has accepted a GATT ruling on a challenge brought by the United States that subsidies paid to EC soya bean producers should be phased out. This will increase imports of US soya beans. The arrangements for opening this market will be negotiated in the Uruguay Round.

There was an additional, common, critical feature about all of these cases. As well as prosecuting all of them through the GATT disputes system, the United States also applied its unilateral trade provisions. In each case the country concerned faced the threat of some form of US unilateral trade retaliation if it did not follow GATT processes. There is no doubt that US bilateral pressure (using the 301 procedures among others) was the primary force to which the government of Japan responded. These are clear cases where the United States has used the leverage under its Trade Act to support the multilateral trade system.

The United States has not on all occasions used its leverage to support results consistent with GATT. It imposed tariffs on imports of Japanese electronic products to retaliate against Japan's reneging, in its view, on the terms of an agreement between the two of them about trade in computer chips (semiconductors). The agreement is a cartel and not consistent with the concept of market forces or prices. The United States also imposed tariffs on imports from Brazil in retaliation for Brazil's refusal to change its intellectual property laws. GATT does not cover intellectual property (this is one of the new areas being negotiated in the Uruguay Round).

The United States has been operating a vigilante system. It is always high risk to take the law into one's own hands. It is claimed that in retaliation for the imposition of the tariffs on Japanese products in the semiconductor dispute Japanese banks delayed their purchases of Treasury Bonds at the next auction so that US interest rates payable on those bonds was one per centage point higher.

The mix of policy impulses in the US approach to international trade is comprehensible if we looks at where the policy pushes come from. To make a generalization, the Reagan and Bush administrations had and have Cabinet officers who are committed to multilateral trade principles. At the same time the United States has had the most protectionist Congress in decades. The basic competition between those two forces explains much, although not all, of the peculiar contradictions in US policy.

The administration was only able to push as hard as it did for the Uruguay Round because it gave some ground to the powerful protectionist forces in Congress. It is one of the serendipities of the Uruguay Round that at the time of its convening and throughout its process all the key Cabinet officers concerned with the trade round, including the president, have basically believed in free trade principles.

The US negotiating agenda

The Reagan and Bush administrations clearly wanted to give GATT a go. Two general strategic options have emerged throughout the 1980s: either revitalization of the multilateral trading system or the creation of a network of free trade arrangements in which North American and trans-Pacific arrangements would feature. A third *de facto* course would be to pursue a general policy of unilateral leverage and retaliation to secure access to markets. The third alternative would be regarded by many in the industry and Congress not as an alternative but as a supplement to either a global multilateral system or a free trade network.

The idea of a superGATT which would be restricted to the OECD countries, plus a few others, has had currency in policy circles in Washington. It is hard to see why this would work. There is really only one problem with GATT: the extent to which the European Community and the United States have chosen to avoid its disciplines. They have done so primarily because of the competitive challenge of Japan and the Asian/Pacific rim economies. These countries will continue to be major US trading partners and would have to be included in any new arrangement if it were to make sense. Latin America is a major US trading partner region. We must presume in the longer run that the debt burdens will be overcome. It would be short-sighted of the United States to place this group outside a trading system in which it operated.

The administration wants the GATT multilateral trading system re-invigorated. The pressure from the new international trading sectors is for international arrangements; and it is the only economically rational course to pursue. If the Uruguay Round does not meet expectations, however, US interest can be expected to focus rapidly elsewhere.

Clayton Yeutter first as USTR and then afterwards, as secretary of agriculture, fixed global liberalization as a key US goal in the trade round. The US administration faces significant domestic resistance to this. Many US agricultural sectors are heavily protected, particularly the dairy and sugar industries. Nearly all others receive significant support in one form or another from Washington. To be acceptable to Congress, any agreement to cut agricultural support has to include tangible commitments from the European Community to liberalize and to wind down use of export subsidies.

The strongest pressure on the administration to achieve liberalization comes from the global services industries. They want access to markets for financial services, telecommunications, construction industries and consultancies. In pushing for a positive result they are joined by companies who want international rules governing intellectual property to be strengthened. These include the pharmaceutical industries, the sound and video recording industry and the computer software industry.

Manufacturing industry in the United States is either generally silent about trade liberalization through the GATT or apprehensive. There are a few activists. Caterpillar is one. It suffers from the protection which the US steel industry enjoys. This makes the steel it purchases for manufacturing more expensive. The automobile industry would not want the current protective arrangements disturbed, although General Motors joined the business MTN Coalition formed in 1990 to support the outcome of the Uruguay Round. The chemical industry has signalled to the administration that tariff cuts should not be contemplated casually.

The strongest opposition in the United States to liberalization is from the US textile and clothing industry. It has made a point of tying down nearly every administration before a multilateral trade negotiation to toughen up or reconfirm the Multi-fibre Arrangement so that it could not be tampered with in negotiations. The textile industry was not able to nail the administration down in 1989 quite as well as it had in the past. Liberalization of the MFA is one of the major items on the agenda in the Uruguay Round negotiations.

Tightening up international rules restricting the use of subsidies was another US objective. There is little enthusiasm for this in the rest of the world. Most countries regard domestic subsidies as right – they are legal under GATT – and usually fail to appreciate the way in which they can inhibit imports. US interests are driven by regular squabbles with Canada over subsidization of Canadian industry as well as concerns about subsidization of the steel and aircraft industries in the European Community.

Clarifying rules on the origin of exports is another area of interest to the United States, which has been watching with mounting concern how the European Community has been re-defining the origin of products as it plays its cat and mouse game through the anti-dumping system to keep Japanese and East Asian products out. The Community is also reviewing these rules as part of the process of rationalizing barriers to imports to create the single market. The United States has warned the Community not to create rules that would hinder the possible export of an automobile manufactured in the United States because the parent company is Japanese.

The United States has a general interest in encouraging the European Community to settle new regulations that arise from the single market in the Uruguay Round. The Community is reviewing rules which affect the rights of foreign owned companies to supply to government agencies and it is setting standards such as health and safety which would affect imports. There are GATT rules governing these areas.

An additional new area into which the United States has pushed the GATT is the restrictive effect on trade of investment measures. The United States has proposed a code which will inhibit the extent to which countries can put trade-related conditions on investment.

The United States also set a general objective of securing a greater commitment among developing countries to GATT disciplines. Many developing countries exercise the right to impose trade restrictions on the grounds that they have balance of payments problems. These rules have become very lax and many developing countries use them for outright protection. In addition, most developing countries have committed ('bound') only a small percentage of their tariff to GATT rules. The US goal was to see developing countries commit to apply GATT rules to more of their tariffs and to restrict the grounds upon which trade barriers could be used for balance of payments reasons.

The bottom line for the United States will be agreements which offer liberalization of trade in agriculture, new disciplines on trade in products with intellectual property components and an agreement as well as initial liberalization of trade in services. It may need to show some outcome in the other areas but Congressional approval of the outcome of the Uruguay Round is unlikely unless the bottom line is reached.

Chapter Six

PAN-EUROPE –
looking inward or outward

Frans Andriessen is known as one of the three liberals among the 17 European Commissioners who took office in 1989. He is a vice-president of the Commission. In 1989 he became the Commissioner responsible for external relations and trade, taking over from Willy de Clercq who led the EC team at Punta del Este in September 1986. Andriessen had also been at Punta, but as the Commissioner with the agriculture portfolio. Ironically, Clayton Yeutter made a similar change in early 1989, but in the opposite direction, swapping the trade portfolio for the agriculture portfolio in the new Bush administration. Andriessen and Yeutter both provided continuity in official policy towards the Uruguay Round in the new administrations in Washington and Brussels. This was very important.

A Dutchman, Andriessen saw through the most important reforms of the Common Agricultural Policy (CAP) in the history of the European Community as Commissioner for Agriculture. The climax of this process was the meeting of the EC Council of Ministers which was held in February 1988. The Council agreed a package of proposals from the Commission for reform of the CAP. The most important feature was that ceilings were imposed on how much money could be spent on the CAP. Cuts in production of some commodities were agreed, as were measures known as 'stabilizers' which triggered cuts once agreed limits were exceeded.

The CAP was the largest single item of expenditure in the EC budget and until 1988 it had regularly run over budget. Securing agreement to the reform package had been a major achievement for Andriessen. While he considered that the Uruguay Round was important there is no question that reform of the CAP budget was his priority in 1987. Part of the terms of agreement to the reform package was that the European Community expected other farm exporters to cut back production as well. It was an objective to secure this recognition in the Uruguay Round.

It was something of a personal disappointment to Andriessen that the Americans and other exporters reacted as coolly as they did to the reforms of the CAP. The Americans did not accept the argument that the EC measures created 'credit' that others now had to match by cutting back their own production. They accepted that the reforms put a lid on production generally but they were concerned that it was porous. They were not convinced that the stabilizers would work.

Trade relations between the United States and the Community had been vexatious and bitter over the previous few years. There had been some major, continuing trade disputes, mostly over agricultural issues. There had been an expensive subsidy war which peaked in 1986/7 and had raised costs and driven down world prices. A trade war in early 1987 over the terms of accession of Spain and Portugal to the European Community was just averted because the Community settled under threat of serious trade retaliation by the US. Andriessen had had to handle all these issues as Commissioner for Agriculture.

The European Community especially disliked the 301 retaliatory procedures in the US Trade Act. By threatening retaliation the Community had succeeded in talking the United States out of including EC measures in the annual list of 'unfair' trading practices which were reported to Congress in 1989. One of the primary interests of the European Community in the Uruguay Round was to secure greater commitment from the United States to use GATT procedures to handle trade disputes rather than resorting to unilateral action under its own trade legislation.

At the beginning of 1989 Andriessen would have regarded securing a successful conclusion to the Round as one of the priority tasks in his new term of office. Another would have been to handle the external dimension of the single market programme. By the end of the year coordinating the response of the West to reform in Eastern Europe was imposed on top of an already crowded agenda. Frans Andriessen was probably confronted with the largest international agenda that any external relations Commissioner had ever had to handle. His job was not only to handle the Community's relations with the rest of the world but also to ensure that the Commission took account of the rest of the world.

EC approaching critical mass

The end of cold war confrontation means that economic integration and collaboration will become more important in European affairs than military alliances. The obligations of the Treaty of Rome, and the limits to sovereignty and restrictions on behaviour that they impose, will determine the conduct of international affairs in Europe. They will supplant the obligations of NATO and the Warsaw Pact as the basic determinants of behaviour among states in Europe.

In addition to the new united Germany, natural EC expansion over the next two decades could include Austria, Norway, Sweden, Switzerland, Finland, Hungary, Czechoslovakia and possibly Poland; but this alone will not explain the greater importance of the European Community. It will arise from the leadership of united Germany, greater executive authority for Brussels and the influence of the single market. The European Community is gaining critical mass.

United Germany and the European Community

Membership by united Germany in the European Community will be the key element of the order in post-Iron Curtain Europe. This will contribute and be seen to be contributing more tangibly to laying the basis for stability in Europe than agreements about security reached between Germany and the 'Four Powers'. After security questions about the relationship of the new Germany to

NATO and to the Warsaw Pact have been sorted out, they will rapidly prove not to have been the major issues.

The consensus that the Germanies could unite emerged very quickly after the communist political order was overturned in Eastern Europe. The end of the hegemony of the Soviet Communist Party swiftly removed the rationale for a divided Germany. The first steps taken to achieve unification point to the significance of what has changed.

Countries do not enter arrangements which involve the surrender of sovereignty while major political or strategic differences exist among them. But in the case of the two Germanies the first action taken towards unification was adoption of a common currency, before merger of armies, before negotiations to settle political differences, and before the drafting of new constitutional arrangements. Union of the currency involves a very significant surrender by one or both parties of economic autonomy. And it happened while each remained a member of a military alliance formed for the purpose of defence against the other.

This is not the most astounding aspect of the emergence of the new order in Europe but it is one of the most fascinating. And it shows clearly how the instruments of economic relations have already become more important than the traditional political/ defence institutions which have been used to shape the politics and international relations in Europe in the modern era.

The current manifestation of these rapidly fading security considerations is the debate about whether Germany will be a member of NATO with part of its territory demilitarized or a neutral state. This is rapidly diminishing in importance as an issue. Once it is consolidated the united Germany will exercise sufficient economic and political power to itself lead the decisions making about what strategic arrangements will apply to the new Germany.

The priorities for the next decade in Europe will be building market economies in Eastern Europe; achieving an orderly transition to pluralist politics in the Soviet Union; and consolidation of democratic and pluralist political institutions in Eastern Europe. As the richest country in Europe, Germany will have a major influence in the 'marketization' of Eastern Europe.

The security sought by some of the larger European countries that a united Germany will not be a threat will be achieved by integrating a united Germany into the European Community, and enhancement of the Community's suprastate role. Within the economic confederation which the European Community will become, Germany will become the leader of Europe. It will be one of the largest countries, but more importantly it will be the largest economy.

Suprastate beginnings

The Community will also move to centre stage in European affairs because it will acquire significant additional executive functions. One of the first responses to the changing situation in Europe was the decision by the OECD countries to pass the responsibility of managing assistance to Eastern European countries to the European Commission.

This was symbolically underlined by Washington's agreement to upgrade the status it accorded the Commission. It had rankled the Commission, and especially President Delors, for years that the United States and others would treat the Commission only as an international organization, not as another state. The general importance of this was small as practical matters went: it generally affected where the EC representative stood in diplomatic reception lines.

The principal executive powers that the Commission exercised on behalf of its member states was administration of trade policy. It is significant that the Commission has been given the job of managing the initial programmes to support economic development in Eastern Europe. It is most likely to be given further supranational authority to administer programmes for the economic reconstruction of Eastern Europe. As part of the response to the challenge of adjusting the mechanisms of the Community to a united Germany, further steps to increase the integration of the members of the European Community will result in the European Commission's acquiring more executive authority than the members have allowed it in the past.

Europe's choice now – member or ally

Whether or not countries in Europe outside the Community join it, all will adopt as a basic reference point how their economic policies relate to EC policies and actions. In other words, their economic policies will either have to be altered to harmonize with EC policies so that they will be acceptable candidates if they want to apply for membership; or their policies will have to harmonize if they want to avoid being excluded from Community markets.

This phenomenon of other Europeans adjusting their policies to internal EC developments is one of the spin offs from the single market exercise. The proposed 'European Economic Space' is the first manifestation. The concept is an agreement between EC and EFTA countries which would enable companies in the EFTA countries to compete in the expanded markets which are being created in the single market programme. It essentially requires the EFTA countries to adopt changes in their own economies to parallel changes being implemented by the EC member states.

The newly 'marketizing' countries of Eastern Europe have stronger incentives to harmonize their domestic economic regimes to the Community. They want EC aid and financial assistance; they need access to the Community markets; and some will aspire to join the European Community – certainly Hungary, Czechoslovakia and Poland.

The greater orientation of other Europeans to the European Community was triggered by the single market. The economies of the EFTA countries were already heavily dependent on the Community. They had no choice but to adjust to the new arrangements created by the single market, and on the Community's terms. The political revolution in Eastern Europe has intensified the importance of greater EC integration. But the key is how creation of the single market affects Europe's attitude to the global economy. Will it encourage Europe to look inward or outward? What value will it attach to global trading arrangements?

EC 92 – bonus and threat

The European Community is in a phase of development that is the most important since the signature of the Treaty of Rome – its foundation stone. This phase has been triggered by the decision in 1985 to launch a programme to remove all barriers to movements of goods, people and services – the creation of a single market. It took the rest of the world a while to realize what the single market exercise meant.

At first it was treated like another of those bureaucratic exercises that the Eurocrats in Brussels were forever dreaming up: something that absorbed a lot of energy in the preparation; that was based on the best principles of an integrated Europe; but that would never be achieved and would occupy hundreds of hours of time of officials. This time the rest of the world were wrong. This project was different and it would become both a bonus and a threat to the multilateral trading system and to the prospects for the Uruguay Round.

Aware of the large number of grand schemes lying unimplemented in Commission reports, the Commission in Brussels decided to approach the single market project a little differently. Led by Lord Cockfield, the Commissioner responsible for the internal market, modern public relations techniques were employed. The Commission sought to create a momentum and to fire the public imagination before any decision was taken to reduce a single barrier. Economic analyses were prepared which concluded that reduction of barriers between the member states would increase growth in the EC by up to 5 per cent. A new era of growth and revitalization was announced. 'The Economist' described it as 'Europhoria'. The period of Eurosclerosis that had set in during the mid-1970s was at an end.

It worked. The expectation of the Euromarket rekindled the enthusiasm for an integrated Europe that had been missing for at least a decade. More importantly, it stimulated business to anticipate the advent of the market and a series of pan - European takeovers and mergers began which were more on the American than European scale. Business had begun to create the single market.

There was, of course, much more to it than a successful public relations campaign. There were substantial underpinnings, one of the most important of which was that the voting system among the EC member states was altered to reduce the extent to which any major change could be held hostage by minority interests.

It took a while before assessments could be made of the relationship between the programme to reduce barriers to trade between the member states of the Community and its involvement in efforts in the Uruguay Round to reduce trade barriers globally. One thing became clear early to the rest of the world. The single market was simply more important to individual member states and to the Commission in Brussels than GATT. 1992, the target date to achieve the single market, is more important than 1990, the conclusion of the Uruguay Round. Until Gorbachev allowed reconstruction in Eastern Europe to begin, the single market was the main event in Europe. It still has top billing.

Top billing

As the EC began the enormous task of preparing the 279 directives to member states to eliminate barriers in areas as diverse as food regulations and accountancy qualifications, the rest of the world suddenly appreciated that this might affect them. The first concern was that the EC was going to build a giant trade and business club that discriminated against companies and business outside. The Americans dubbed it 'Fortress Europe'.

Clearly any move to protectionism by the Community while the Uruguay Round was in progress would undermine the multilateral trade negotiations. There were grounds for concern. Protectionist sentiment in parts of the European Community had always been strong. Reciprocity became a key approach. While the United States was calling for fair trade rather than free trade, the Community was calling for reciprocity instead of free trade. Some EC leaders had declared early on that companies outside Europe were only going to get access to the new, enlarged EC single market if similar opportunities for access were extended to European companies in other markets. This did not square with the GATT approach of providing equal access to all other GATT parties.

The Americans applied significant pressure to the Community. The proposed banking directive to create a single EC banking market would discriminate against American banks. The United States warned the Community that any inclination to restrict the entry to cars built in the United States by Japanese-owned companies would cause serious difficulties. It pressed for arrangements so that American business concerns might be taken into account as directives were being prepared.

EC leaders protested that the purpose of the single market had been misread. But they took the complaints seriously. The offending banking directive was modified somewhat and EC leaders began to allay the fears of 'Fortress Europe'. It took nearly two years, but the fears that the Community would create a crude preferential market receded. US businesses operating in Europe set up an office in Brussels to monitor the preparation of single market directives and concluded on balance that the single market programme was stimulating pressure to increase competitiveness and would be good for business.

There were still some significant acid tests about whether aspects of the programme would have protectionist effects. Would the European Community enshrine reciprocity as a basis for entry by non-EC companies into the financial services area? Would this undermine efforts to liberalize financial services on a global basis in the Uruguay Round? And would some of the more intractable, ancient quotas on imports applied by member states be replaced with a single quota for the EC?

A key issue which is now being closely watched is whether or not new rules may emerge which will control access by foreign companies to the European Community through investment rules. In US trade circles there is concern that the single market might still lead to an 'investment' Fortress Europe. EC officials are showing a distinct inclination to manage anti-dumping policy to require Japanese companies which want to do business in Europe to invest in Europe and to reduce to a minimum the per centage of components imported for manufacturing processes.

In the last year of the Uruguay Round the judgement of the rest of the international community was that efforts in the Uruguay Round to open up international markets would not be undermined by the closing of markets within a 'Fortress Europe' while the Round was under way. The problem which the single market presents for the multilateral trade negotiations is a lot simpler. The single market diverts attention from the Uruguay Round. Major change in economic and trade policies is difficult to achieve. It requires abnormal efforts from officials and politicians. There is a limit to how many abnormal demands can be loaded into political and administrative processes.

Presidents, prime ministers and ministers in the European Community will have their hands full coping with the need to give attention to the issues thrown up by the economic and political restructuring of Europe, the major unresolved Single Market issues, and greater integration of the Community, in addition to the need to attend to the normal issues of the day. The Uruguay Round faces major competition for attention. This is why it was important that President Bush focussed attention on the Round at the Houston Economic Summit in July 1990.

Multilateral agreements to liberalize trade are commitments to reduce domestic levels of protection. International negotiations cannot succeed unless governments enter those negotiations disposed to reduce trade barriers, or prepared to move to such a disposition during the negotiations. The Community did not enter the Uruguay Round enthusiastically. The traditional free traders, the United Kingdom and the Dutch, were keen. The French were not. They considered that ECs agricultural policies would come under fire. The Community would be forced to reduce protection of agriculture and there would be little for the Community to gain. The other member states ranged between these positions. So the Community supported the Round but just below the surface there were doubts that the effort might not be worth the result.

Reducing protection is rarely easy. Wherever there is a barrier of any significance, some domestic producer or holder of an import licence or quota will be benefiting. Governments usually find that the most effective means of reducing protection is to set long-term goals which are not changeable. Industry will always adjust to the inevitable. Industry has to be brought to accept that change is required.

The programme to create the single market has prepared European industry for change. The Commission has surprised member states with the tenacity it has shown recently in trying to enforce greater respect for competition in markets. The principles of the Single European Act mean that no member state can maintain national quotas or subsidies. This is one of the more controversial areas of the single market. It is not likely that all of the measures that should be eliminated will be eliminated. But some will be.

In some areas, anticipation of the need to be more competitive has conditioned companies to potential acceptance of multilateral commitments to reduce protection. Preparation for freedom of movement of services within the Community has conditioned EC industry to the idea of liberalization of trade in services, particularly in financial services, telecommunications and transport.

The positive impact of the Single Market has therefore generally been to put industry in a mood for change and anticipation of the need to be more competitive. This potentially puts the Community in a position where it participates in the Uruguay Round negotiations from a dynamic base. Even those who consider that the Community should insist on reciprocal access for foreign companies which will benefit from the expanded single market regard the Uruguay Round as the occasion to extract trade concessions in return.

The EC negotiating agenda

A fundamental EC interest in the Uruguay Round would be to ensure that agreements reached in it complemented and did not run contrary to the objectives of creating the Single Market and greater economic integration. This interest is basically passive but it has directly influenced some EC positions. The most direct will be towards the services negotiations. The Community wants a GATT agreement which will liberalize trade in services. From the outset it will be looking for commitments which improve access to markets for financial services, value-added telecommunications and transport services.

The disposition to make reciprocity a condition for access to the new services markets in the Community could present serious problems for efforts to negotiate an international services agreement based on liberal principles. The key liberal GATT principle is that when access is granted to a market that same access should be extended on common terms to all members of the agreement.

To establish the single market the Community is creating new pan-EC rules to embrace government procurement, standards for products and rules of origin which determine how much of the origins of a product are EC and how much is foreign. These areas are also under review in the Uruguay Round negotiations and obviously the Community's negotiating positions will clearly be based on what is evolving as single market directives are being settled. The Uruguay Round is an opportunity for EC rules and international GATT rules to be harmonized.

Some aspects of the clearing away of national barriers within the Community will enable it to meet its GATT obligations better. For example, a number of member states have maintained old quantitative restrictions which were not legal under GATT. A number of these are being cleared by the creation of the single market.

An area of active interest to the Community is the intellectual property negotiations. After a slow start EC drug companies and the luxury goods industry are keen for new international rules to be formulated which will provide stronger copyright, trademark and patent protection, and will create international enforcement of these rules. They have created an international alliance with counterpart bodies in the United States and Japan. This is one of the areas in which European industry has articulated clear objectives.

Given the extent to which the greater part of the trade of EC member states is among themselves and with trading partners with which they have preferential agreements, some commentators suggest that the Community's primary interest in GATT is as an instrument to deal with trade relations with the United States. It is a key EC objective to secure a stronger commitment by the United States to a strengthened GATT dispute settlement system and to allow the 301 provisions of the US Trade Act to lapse. The Community is itself prepared to go some way to strengthening the jurisdiction of the GATT dispute settlement system as an enticement.

The Community formally supports liberalization of the

Multi-fibre Arrangement (MFA) which regulates trade in textiles and clothing. Significant parts of EC industry, particularly in Germany and Italy, are internationally competitive. Its approach to reform is piecemeal, however. It has suggested gradual liberalization of existing MFA rules. One reason is extreme caution in Spain and Portugal towards liberalization. Spanish and Portuguese clothing and textiles for consumption in the rest of the Community have become important growth industries. Access to the EC market by more competitive developing countries is severely restricted by the MFA.

The Community strongly opposed the approach to reform suggested by the United States and Canada. Their idea was that each country should replace current restrictions on imports from developing countries which are sanctioned under the MFA with a single quota which covered all imports. These global quotas would be progressively expanded until they disappeared. This would mean that EC exporters would initially have to compete with others for a share of the quota of imports allowed into the US market.

A key objective of the Community, as for the United States, is to see greater commitment to the multilateral trading system by the developing countries. This means reducing their scope to impose trade barriers on the grounds of balance of payments problems and a greater degree of binding of developing country tariffs into GATT disciplines.

Agriculture is the most difficult issue for the Community and the one in which it will be under the most pressure. EC interests in agriculture are both positive and negative. Its officials see the Uruguay Round as an opportunity to secure international agreements that will place general restrictions on how much others, particularly the Americans, spend on agriculture. At a minimum this would assist the Commission to resist pressures from their own farmers to loosen the restrictions on production that were agreed in 1988. They would also like to see the scope for subsidy competition with the Americans in international markets reduced.

There are also disparities between levels and types of support for individual commodities under the CAP. Some products enter the Community duty free, for example soya beans and feed stock. Most imports face very high duties, some of which effectively prevent any trade. The Commission wants to 're-balance', that is raise, some of these low tariffs so that there is less variation between them. The tariffs of greatest interest are bound under GATT rules and the Community could only alter them in the context of a broader negotiation covering a range of subjects where there could be some give and take. It wants to do this in the Uruguay Round.

On the other hand, the Community does not want to go too far down the reform path. There is now greater reference in Commission policy to the role markets can play in determining the patterns of production and trade. But for most of the Community this is revolutionary, especially to German farmers. They are the most inefficient in the Community and they are politically influential in Germany. In the face of pressures from the United States and the Cairns Group to liberalize substantially the EC position is defensive.

As the reunification of Germany has added a significant dimension to EC integration, Germany will play a central role in shaping the Community's final position on the outcome of the Uruguay Round and thereby the success of the Round. How far it can go in the direction of agricultural reform will determine the success or otherwise of efforts to liberalize international trade. Opposition of German farmers will have to be overcome to secure agreement to liberalize agricultural trade. There will be scope for high drama.

Chapter Seven
JAPAN, TIGERS AND THE PACIFIC

Japan has only started to exercise an influence in GATT commensurate with its trade weight since the mid–1980s. It, the United States and the European Community are the big three in world trade. Until recently, it has been the United States and the European Community which appear to have exercised preponderant influence. When the Uruguay Round negotiations began, Japan claimed its place. While the Americans had put trade related investment measures on the table of the negotiations, Japan provided the presiding officer of that negotiating group. Given the way Japan had emerged as giant capital exporter, this was particularly appropriate.

Ambassador Tomohiko Kobayashi was a well known Japanese diplomat in international circles. He had been prominent in economic debates in the UN General Assembly and was widely respected, including among developing countries. When appointed as chairman of the negotiating group he was ambassador for the multilateral trade negotiations, a Tokyo-based position with responsibility for international discussions on multilateral trade issues.

Kobayashi was urbane. He knew Europe, having studied as a student in the Bourgogne. He brought a very professional approach to the work of the negotiating group on trade-related investment measures (TRIMs) and this was the trouble. This issue was even more unpopular with the developing countries than either services or intellectual property. Most of them had

tight restrictions on foreign investment which they did not wish
to see circumscribed and they did not wish to concede that
conditions attached to investment might have a bearing on
trade. Their position was that GATT was silent on investment
and that things should stay that way. They did not want
anything to happen in this group.

In the period after the Montreal mid-term review TRIMs
became a subject in which proper negotiations began. This was
a tribute to the quiet persistence with which Kobayashi kept the
negotiating group focused on the issue. This was an important
area to Japan. It was facing an increasing array of conditions on
investment from the European Community and in addition
Japanese investment was extensive throughout the Asian/Pacific
region. It had financed a lot of growth there and would continue
to do so.

The Pacific century

The idea that the twenty-first century will be the Pacific century
fired imaginations in the late 1980s. The Pacific rim was seen as
having the right combination of capital, sustained growth,
dynamism, resources, technology and markets for developments
in the region to dominate the affairs of the century. When Asian/
Pacific governments met in Canberra in November 1989 to
inaugurate regional economic cooperation, James Baker, US
Secretary of State, declared that the meeting would be as
seminal to the future as the post-war meetings at Bretton Woods
had been to the development of the post-war international
economic system.

Trade growth in the region has been typified by several
developments:

1. Average rates of growth among countries of the region
   have been higher compared with other regions for two
   decades (see Figure 7.1).
2. Trade was a key component of growth strategies.
3. Japan had emerged as a major trader and had a
   commanding influence in trade of certain products.

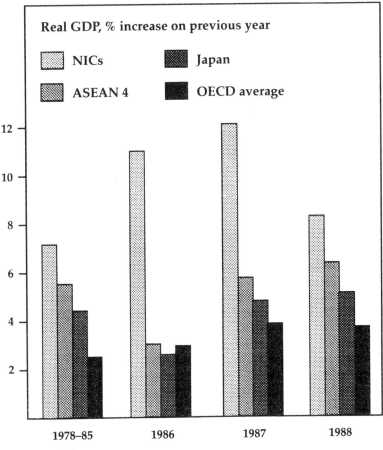

FIGURE 7.1 *Asian/Pacific growth*

4. Other countries in the region had also started to emerge as major traders in their own right.

This pattern seems set. In 1988 the World Bank chanced its arm and predicted GDP growth between 1987 and 1995 for industrialized countries between 2.3 and 3.0 per cent, compared to growth for developing country exporters of manufactures (this would be predominantly the Asian/Pacific countries) at between 5.0 and 6.5 per cent for the same period.

All predictions are hazardous. It is likely that reconstruction of Eastern Europe will increase the growth rate among EC economies, particularly Germany. There are some uncertainties. The pressure for redistribution of wealth in the Asian/Pacific economies will intensify as democratic institutions consolidate. As labour costs rise, will these economies adjust to maintain competitiveness and move to higher levels of value-added production?

Another significant uncertainty is China. Will the Hong Kong economy be allowed to function at the same hectic pace after it is formally incorporated into China in 1997? Will relations between Taipei and Beijing thaw to permit greater Taiwanese investment in China? Will China be able to contribute consistently to growth in the region? It can be expected to remain in its current economic slump until the middle of the 1990s. There will be significant growth in the region without steady development in China: there will be much greater growth if there is steady growth in China.

Basic forces are at work in the Asia/Pacific societies which suggest continued aggressive growth. The objective of striving to raise the standards of living to those enjoyed in the industrialized countries is an important spur. This is the declared objective of many governments in the region, even to surpass the Western standards. In the next century the Confucian ethic may supplant the Protestant ethic as the premier basis for building prosperity.

The global pattern of trade has already been influenced by the emergence of Japan; it is now being further influenced by the new group of international traders from the Pacific rim. They have presented fresh challenges to the trans-Atlantic trading order upon which GATT is based. The European Community has started to employ its anti-dumping procedures against exports from Korea, Hong Kong and Taiwan and the United States has started to subject them to its 301 procedures.

These countries want most of all an open, global trading system. The global trading system must accommodate them if it is to have any value. A global multilateral trading system is the only efficient economic option available. Geopolitics suggests other, much less satisfactory, possibilities if the GATT system cannot meet their interests.

History, investment, education and trade patterns reveal a

common Pacific interest. Most of the foreign investment in the region is American or Japanese. The primary trading partners of countries in the region are the United States, Japan and increasingly other countries in the region. There is a perception that the European Community is protectionist and not a natural trading or investment partner. The talk of Fortress Europe has stimulated debate about economic cooperation among the Asian/Pacific economies. At the Canberra meeting to discuss regional economic cooperation in 1989 all participants stressed that an overriding objective was multilateral trade liberalization. They wanted to give GATT a go first.

Japan – too competitive

Japan's growth as a world trader has been spectacular. It and Germany are frequently compared, properly so. In fact Japan's economic recovery began later than Germany's. Japan's success as an exporter stimulated a lot of the protectionist actions taken by the industrialized countries in the 1960s and 1970s. A number of these actions were responsible for effectively removing significant areas of trade from the GATT multilateral trading system.

An important difference between Japan and Germany was Germany's openness to imports. It has been consistently claimed through the 1980s in the United States and Europe that Japan's low share of imports was a major reason for the imposition of restrictions on its exports. The primary reason for restrictions on Japanese exports was because they were too competitive.

It would appear that imports of manufactures into Japan are now starting to rise. This is from a very low base but it may be the beginning of a significant trend. The Bush administration has begun to concede that the imbalance of trade between the United States and Japan is predominantly a function of the US budget deficit and the view is emerging that Japanese trade barriers may contribute about 20 per cent of the trade imbalance. Belief in the impenetrability of Japanese trade barriers is still strong in Congress and Europe, however.

Until the late 1980s Japan was more the hunted prey of the

United States and the European Community rather than trading partner. The cheapness of Japanese exports of textiles in the 1950s caused the first formal restriction of international trade in textiles to be registered in GATT. This was imposed as a condition of Japan's accession to the GATT in 1955. In time this arrangement became extended as developing countries industrialized and also became more competitive exporters of textiles than the industrialized countries.

As Japan developed exports of steel, electronic consumer goods and motor vehicles, these too became subject to barriers or restraints on entry into most European countries and the United States. Since the late 1960s there has been a nearly relentless pattern of American and European trade barriers and restrictions levied against Japanese imports. The fact that most of them were arrangements not recognized in GATT which, while not technically illegal, were certainly contrary to the liberal economics of the GATT, is testimony to the fact that this was a general rearguard action against superior Japanese competitiveness.

Until the mid-1980s, Japan chose not to meet these American and European assaults head on. Usually when asked to agree to some form of restriction – a voluntary restraint on exports, administrative guidance to exporters or compliance with forecasts of exports – Japanese industry and officialdom went along. Japanese industry quietly persisted by developing new products, seeking local partners and constantly improving products.

Imports of manufactures had a small share of the domestic Japanese market. European and American industrialists complained that this was deliberate policy. Japanese officials contended that European and American exporters did not make nearly the same effort as Japanese exporters to research foreign markets, to take account of consumer tastes, to concentrate on creating a high quality product and to understand how markets operated.

In private Japanese officials were able to make these points in a telling way. At one conference in England in the mid-1980s, after having been regaled by a Gerran for twenty minutes about Japanese protectionism, an official from Gaimusho (the Japanese foreign ministry) wondered if it were symptomatic of the European approach to doing business in Japan that in the mid-

1980s there were more European priests living in Japan than businessmen.

In response to this pressure, formal Japanese import barriers were reduced. Perhaps with the confidence this gave, as well as the rapid growth in the value of Japanese capital, Japan started to behave somewhat more assertively over international trade issues. When challenged with threatening action the Japanese have begun to dig in. In GATT Japan has taken the initiative and lodged complaints against the European Community and the United States. Japan recently won its first case in GATT against EC penalties imposed for what the Community claimed was circumvention of anti-dumping duties on photocopiers and other items which were being manufactured in factories in the Community.

Japan's negotiating agenda

Japan's first objective in supporting the Uruguay Round was to head off protectionism in the US Congress. In the mid-1980s the chance of Congress imposing some across the board import barriers was high. It remains an abiding Japanese interest that the United States chooses to support an international set of trade rules rather than acting unilaterally to meet its trade objectives. Japan would be prepared to pay for such an outcome.

Japan has also a broad interest in strengthening arrangements which reduce the opportunity for others, particularly the European Community and to a lesser extent the United States, to discriminate against Japanese trade and investment. Japan has joined with the other East Asian economies to press for tighter disciplines governing the use of anti-dumping procedures, particularly by the European Community. Japan would also like clarification of the rules of origin which are used to determine local content requirements for imports and manufactures using imported components, as well as an international set of rules governing trade-related investment measures. Many countries put conditions on investment which are designed to influence import or export patterns.

Japan shares the interest of the United States and the

European Community in strong trade rules for items with intellectual property content. It has made strong statements in favour of liberalization of trade in services but has not clearly defined its interests. Presumably these will be driven by the relative degree of deregulation of Japanese services industries.

Protection of its agricultural sector is the issue over which Japan is the most defensive. This is the most sensitive issue for it in the negotiations. The Liberal Democratic government had agreed under pressure from the United States and others in GATT to open up the Japanese beef market. To defend high import barriers on rice Japan has argued the need for special exceptions. The United States and the Cairns Group subjected Japan to heavy pressure to agree to liberalize further. Japan can be expected to take its cue on this issue from the European Community.

Japan has not taken the same strong position as the United States and European Community on the need for developing countries to commit themselves to GATT disciplines. This is partly out of strategic regard for Japan's long term relationships with developing countries in the Asian/Pacific region. It is also significant that in many of them export industries are financed with Japanese capital.

Tigers and dragons

As the delegates ground on into their sixth consecutive early morning session in mid-July 1985, negotiating the draft declaration for the Punta del Este launch of the trade negotiations, Felipe Jaramillo from Colombia attempted again to summarize the position. For four hours there had been circular discussion of relatively straightforward language on safeguards – the rules governing imposition of emergency protection against surges of damaging, fairly priced imports. The Korean ambassador, Kun Park, had twice requested that a point be included. Most of the time had been taken up with some of the older Geneva hands spinning out the time on peripheral issues.

Kun Park had not been in Geneva long. Even so, he had served as chairman of the GATT council and had won wide respect. Jaramillo made a last effort to sum up. Before he had finished reading out his summary of the negotiating text, there was a loud crash from the back of the room, followed by the sound of tinkling glass. The room hushed. Kun Park had smashed his fist on the desk and the water glass had fractured. 'Why have you not taken into account my point!', he exclaimed. 'You have taken account of the positions of all these others who speak for ages. My government asked me to have the point included. I insist that it is.'

Park was right. He had not argued on at repetitive length like the others. Koreans are businesslike and to the point. Yet Jaramillo had inadvertently overlooked his point. Others might have relented, considering that they had tried. But the Koreans had important trade interests at stake. They would ensure that their interests would be reflected. This was one of the new features of the changing GATT.

The Koreans were part of the Asian/Pacific economies that needed the same open environment for trade and growth as GATT created for the European economies immediately after the Second World War. If the locus of activity of GATT could be shifted around the globe like the footprint of a geostationary satellite, it needed to be shifted from the Atlantic to the Pacific.

Growth in the Asian/Pacific region had been high, steady and solidly based on trade. For the last two decades, the Asian NIEs and the ASEAN countries had posted consistently better rates of growth than the average for the OECD countries. South Korea and Taiwan appeared to be following the Japanese pattern of progressively shifting production to more hi-tech and capital intensive manufacturing and investing, with Japan, in the lower wage cost ASEAN countries to manufacture lower cost items there.

There was also a significant trend to liberalization of economies among all the countries of the region. Some of them were at critical points in their development. South Korea and Taiwan were wavering between opening their economies fully or maintaining heavily managed segments, as Japan did. Hong Kong and Singapore had completely open economies, although the Singapore government had a wide array of measures to encourage investment in trade exposed sectors. Access to the US market had been a key component in the growth strategies among these countries. All had built sizable trade surpluses with the United States. So far only Korea and Taiwan had been subject to the sort of restraints that the United States imposed on Japanese exports, but to a lesser extent. All feared imposition of trade barriers by a protectionist Congress.

Key supporters of the Round

In a key sense the Uruguay Round is the Pacific Round. When the United States started advocating a new trade round, its first supporters were Japan, the smaller industrialized countries and some of the Latin Americans, mainly the agricultural exporters. The European Community was ambivalent.

There were two initial reactions from the developing countries. There were those who said a round would be alright provided that new issues like services were not included and that the burden to liberalize fell on those who had closed markets to developing countries (i.e. the United States and the European Community); and there were those who were silent. The Asian/ Pacific developing countries were initially in this latter category and uneasy about it. They went along with all the concerns expressed by their developing country friends but at the same time were increasingly worried about the threat of rising protectionism in the United States.

In 1985 the Pacific rim developing countries moved decisively to actively support the convening of a new trade round including, despite reservations, the issues of services and intellectual property. The ASEAN group, whose spokesman at that time was the feisty ambassador from Singapore, Chew Tai Soo, played a critical role in this shift.

This reflected a major interest which differentiated them from most other developing countries. They had major trade interests. They had become major international traders in manufactured goods. They were going to move their interests and shift the established balance of forces in GATT permanently to align it with international trade flows. This was to be one of the seminal underpinnings of the Uruguay Round.

What the tigers wanted

The overriding aim of the Asian Pacific tigers was a renewed commitment by the United States and the European Community to multilateral trading principles. The economic future of these countries rests on markets being open and having a chance to compete. The Round represented a major opportunity to press the European Community to ease the restrictions it has started to put in place through anti-dumping rules on exports from the East Asian economies.

Hong Kong and Korea are major textile exporters. They support liberalization of the Multi-fibre Arrangement. There are areas of trade in this sector which these countries would lose to other efficient developing country exporters with liberalization. Nevertheless, their industries are highly developed commercially and would adjust readily to changing markets. Indonesia and the Philippines would press for any liberalization to be gradual.

An interesting area in which these countries have cooperated to advance negotiating proposals is on arrangements for emergency protection (safeguards). All are very concerned that there should not be agreements allowing individual countries to restrict imports from other individual countries if there is a damaging, but fairly priced surge of imports. The European Community has been keen on getting such an approach legitimized in the GATT for years.

Interests in services are mixed. Hong Kong and Singapore see benefits for their economies in liberalization of services. Other countries in the region are wary. There is general support for an agreement on trade-related intellectual property rules, but not necessarily for rules as tight as proposed by the United States and the European Community. There is a defensive interest in supporting an international instrument as an alternative to continuation of the pressure which the United States has applied bilaterally to most countries in the region in recent years.

All countries expect to be pressed by the trading majors to lower tariffs and bind them to GATT disciplines. Tariff levels in the region are high on average and all are prepared for such a negotiation. Increased access to the markets of the European Community in particular, and to a lesser extent to Japan, for exports of tropical products is an important objective of the ASEAN countries.

The Asian/Pacific economies will be defensive about surrender of some of the rights that developing countries have to avoid full application of some GATT disciplines. Privately some of them concede that, as the levels of affluence in their economies rise, they will not be able to claim special treatment on the grounds that they are developing countries. However, they will leave the running on this to the other developing countries which have a stronger vested interest in maintaining these rights.

Chaper Eight

THIRD WORLD– CHANGING PERSPECTIVES

Late in 1985 Shri Rang Shukla, the Indian ambassador to GATT, introduced a paper at a meeting of the GATT council which set out the attitude of the group of developing countries in GATT to the idea of a new round of trade negotiations. Shukla was the lawyer's diplomat. Even when he spoke off the cuff it was as if he were drafting a legally watertight statement. Every sentence was carefully crafted, usually including a number of clauses to ensure that no shades of position were ignored and that all ts were crossed. He always politely but firmly insisted that he be permitted to spell out the detail of his positions.

India had been the coordinator of the developing countries in GATT for several years. The group did not operate in a highly structured way and on the occasions when it did produce a common position this was usually based on work done by one of its leading members such as India or Brazil. Many of the diplomats from developing countries who represented their country's interest in GATT also attended UNCTAD meetings. UNCTAD was basically controlled by the developing countries and positions adopted there were often drawn on when positions were formulated in GATT. The Indians had always been active in UNCTAD.

The statement delivered by Shukla had been cleared through the developing country group. It was firmly rooted in the orthodoxy of developing country attitudes about trade liberalization which had been built up over the years. Developing countries in principle supported a trade round. But there were a number of conditions. The industrialized countries were responsible for the major distortions of international trade; it was up to them to act to remove them; developing countries should not be asked to liberalize as part of this process; the special development needs of developing countries should be recogized; areas of priority for liberalization were textiles, agriculture, tropical products and safeguards.

There was a discordant note in the statement. The idea that negotiations to liberalize trade in services might have a place in any trade round was rejected outright. The statement asserted that GATT set rules for trade in goods, not services. For several years the Americans had been pushing for inclusion of services in a new round; it was clear that it was a basic US requirement. In diplomatic parlance, therefore, this statement was negative towards the convening of a round.

While the Indians and some others, like Brazil and Egypt, were comfortable with this statement, others, particularly those who were heavily dependent on trading into the US market, were a bit uneasy. They also did not like services but they attached importance to getting a trade round launched. A number had national programmes of liberalization in train and were relaxed about being required to liberalize themselves. Overall they had doubts about the merit of being uncompromising. Attitudes among developing countries have always been diverse but a rift was in prospect. India would not deliver another comprehensive statement on the round on behalf of all developing countries.

A strong statement of claims

The Uruguay Round is the first multilateral trade negotiation in which developing countries have participated wholeheartedly. They helped shape its agenda, they bargained over the political compact which underpins it and they have helped keep it on course. In previous trade rounds developing countries tended to sit back to leave the running to the industrialized countries. This is the first round in which the developing counties have agreed to submit trade and tariff data to the GATT database which is used for the negotiations to reduce tariffs.

The Uruguay Round is as important as the efforts in the mid-1970s in the aftermath of the Arab oil embargoes to negotiate international economic arrangements to solve the economic problems of the North and South. Those efforts were futile. The current round has a much better chance of success. It is balanced on a much more evenly weighted set of interests between developed and developed countries.

The industrialized countries want new international agreements to liberalize trade in services and to establish trade rights in intellectual property. Annual trade in these sectors is worth over US$600 billion. Most of this is conducted by the industrialized countries and represents around 25 per cent of their global exports. The developing countries want liberalization of trade in agriculture and clothing and textiles. Annual trade in these sectors is worth over US$400 billion of which about US$120 billion is developing country trade – about 25 per cent of total exports from developing countries. One set of interests will not be satisfied without agreement to satisfy the other.

But the Uruguay Round differs importantly from the efforts in the 1970s because the issues are not all polarized across a North/ South divide. There are important areas where there is concurrence among developed and developing countries that liberalization should generally occur. In some areas proposals for liberalization were jointly sponsored by developing countries. In agriculture efficient exporters in developed and developing countries are arrayed together against the United States, the European Community and Japan.

A desultory North–South dialogue

Collaboration between developed and industrialized countries was difficult to accept for those who were accustomed to countries always lining up on either side of the North/South divide. Negotiations in the late 1969s and the 1970s over international economic issues were like trench warfare.

In 1964 the UN Conference on Trade and Development was created. Its developing country founders aspired to create a body which would coordinate all economic activity in the UN and the related specialized bodies where it concerned developing countries. UNCTAD became a forum for confrontation between developed and developing countries. Even when there was no cause for confrontation, UNCTAD's decision making procedures created an adversarial environment. Before a decision on any matter was taken the developing countries adopted a group position and likewise the developed countries. Final decisions were arrived at by accommodation of those two positions. But the group positions themselves were compromises among the diverse interests of countries in each group and further accommodation was difficult. The process itself generated intransigence and inflexibility.

A view about development evolved in UNCTAD that developing countries could not industrialize to compete with industrialized countries and developing countries would continue to rely on exports of commodities. The development prescription popularized by the UNCTAD was that it was incumbent on the North to provide aid, to provide access for exports from the South on preferred terms, and that the South was entitled to use protection to support its economies. Global trade liberalization was regarded as a plaything of the rich and GATT was derided as a rich man's club. The slogan 'Trade not Aid' was regarded as an approach designed to divert attention from the obligation of the rich North to increase aid.

UNCTAD was a deliberate body. Apart from being a forum for discussing ideas its concrete achievements were modest. One concrete trade benefit for developing countries to emerge from UNCTAD was the Generalized System of Trade Preferences. Under it industrialized countries were encouraged to offer margins of preference in their tariffs to imports from developing countries. Most industrialized countries introduced preferences but they were on the whole modest. The tendency was not to offer cuts on items in which the developing country concerned was competitive.

When the Arab oil exporters organized a cartel and dramatically lifted oil prices in the early 1970s, and embargoed all oil shipments during the Middle East War, it seemed that the developing countries at last had some economic muscle with which to bargain. In 1974 a declaration of a New International Economic Order was adopted in the United Nations. Much of the UNCTAD philosophy was enshrined in it but little resulted. International conferences were organized in Paris for negotiations between North and South. The North wanted assurances of energy supplies. The South's agenda was development. Little concrete emerged. Work began on an international Common Fund to introduce stability into trade in commodities.

Trade – commodity arrangements

Consistent with the prevailing philosophy of development, trade liberalization was not generally regarded as an obligation of developing countries. Along with providing aid, liberalization was what the industrialized countries had to do. The correctness of this would have seemed borne out by the progressive tightening of restrictions by industrialized countries on imports of clothing and textiles from the developing world. In the late 1960s and early 1970s developing countries were generally encouraged therefore to adopt a passive attitude to participation in the GATT.

The international emphasis on trade in UNCTAD was on managing trade in commodities. UNCTAD had long encouraged international commodity arrangements. Most commodity exporters were developing countries, most commodity importers were industrialized countries. The Common Fund was to bankroll commodity funds to even out fluctuations in prices and to keep the export earnings of the developing countries high and stable. The United States was totally opposed to the Common Fund. It was against the manipulation of prices of commodities. West Germany was also strongly opposed.

The Tokyo Round was begun in 1973 and then dragged on in fits and starts and, after a concentrated effort in 1979, concluded. The attitudes of the developing countries mirrored to a large extent what was going on in the UN and UNCTAD. The major contribution of the developing countries to the Tokyo Round was to negotiate a general statement of lesser obligation of developing countries to liberalize than the industrialized countries. This is known as Part IV of GATT.

In some ways they could not be blamed for this. They had hardly been encouraged to participate in the Tokyo Round. The industrialized countries would not put on the table the trade sectors of interest to the developing countries and in which there were the greatest barriers – agriculture and clothing and textiles. And finally the idea that it was in their own interests to participate in the negotiations in order to make their own economies more efficient had currency among technocrats in only a few developing countries. It had little enough currency in the industrialized countries.

The collapse of the International Tin Agreement in 1985 leaving US$750 million of bad debts spelt the end of the respectability of commodity arrangements. The effort of the Hunt brothers in Texas to try to corner the silver market ought to have been a timely reminder about the hazards of trying to manipulate markets. The Tin Agreement was the only functioning commodity agreement with stocks to enable its managers to move in and out of the market. But one or two major countries were not in the agreement and some inside it were trading around it. Its collapse was one of the largest commercial defaults in the world. After four years of legal wrangling members of the agreement agreed to pay creditors US$300 million in an out of court settlement.

Given this, it is bizarre that following the collapse of the Tin Agreement and a swing in the international mood away from commodity arrangements and managed markets steps have since been taken to set up the Common Fund. US opposition to the Fund has not diminished but West Germany decided to support it in the early 1980s. The proposal languished until 1988, just short of the number of votes necessary, according to its constitution, to enable it to be implemented. One consequence of perestroika was that the Soviet Union decided to ratify the agreement. The Common Fund will never perform the role originally intended as stockpile banker; but it could become a practical source of technical assistance for developing countries on the development and marketing of commodities.

Participating in GATT

Developing countries have not assumed many GATT obligations. This has been less a function of the general right to special treatment than of the fact that there had not been much pressure on them to do so. For most developing countries only a low percentage of tariffs are bound, whereas 80 to 90 per cent of the tariffs of industrialized countries are bound.

A binding is generally made after a bilateral negotiation to reduce the tariff. It is a commitment not to raise the tariff. Most reductions of tariffs are undertaken with the principal supplier of the import or with whomever the original negotiation was conducted. Most of the time the major trading partner is another major trader. And under the GATT rules when there is agreement to lower the tariff all other GATT members benefit.

So most minor traders, which most developing countries are in comparison with the industrialized traders, do not have to participate in many one to one negotiations to reduce tariffs to enjoy the benefits of tariff reductions. It is open to them to contribute to the process generally by unilaterally binding their tariffs. And this will be suggested to many in the Uruguay Round tariff negotiations.

Until the Uruguay Round developing countries did not even submit data on their tariffs to the GATT secretariat which maintains a tariff database. In the past that database has contained only information on the tariff of industrialized countries. A large number of developing countries have agreed to supply information to it.

A number of developing countries have also made wide use of the right in GATT to impose restrictions on trade to help handle balances of payment problems. Something of a controversy has developed over this issue. Industrialized countries generally believe that these provisions are overused, that many restrictions have been left in place for protectionist reasons and that the provisions should be tightened up.

Some developing countries no doubt find it handy to use the grounds of special treatment to evade GATT obligations. There is protection in developing countries. The profit and influence to be won from government protection is not an ideological phenomenon. There have been deliberate policies of economic autarchy and self-sufficiency at various times in India, Brazil and Argentina, for example. And for some adoption of market mechanisms can be extremely difficult. Some developing countries also have elaborate programmes to subsidize basic essentials. Efforts to adjust these programmes so that they are market driven can put governments out of office.

All developing countries would still subscribe to the position that the special needs of developing countries need to be provided for and than none of the measures that recognizes them – the general statement in Part IV of the GATT or the balance of payments provisions – should be changed. However, a significant number of developing countries now accept that they should accept a greater range of GATT obligations to liberalize. This is a reflection of changed attitudes to development.

Liberalization

Through the 1970s, the East Asian economies recorded steady growth in output and in trade. The major sectors of trade in which they had had consistent growth were textiles and clothing, electronics and light manufactures. Their stake in the international trading system was becoming considerable. Their growth depended on the US market. The ASEAN economies were also recording significant, steady growth, as were a number of economies in Latin America. Appreciation spread among the managers of these economies that to enable their economies to develop further, the degree of regulation and protection had to be reduced. A number of countries began domestic programmes to reduce regulation and cut trade barriers.

The build up of debt in the Latin American countries has also had an impact on attitudes to trade liberalization. Initial action on the debt problem has to be taken in the financial institutions and the banking sector. But the capacity of these countries to trade is critical to their ability to pay. There is also wider support within many Latin American countries for liberalization of economies to lay a new a basis for growth. Mexico and Chile have undertaken significant programmes of liberalization. In

1989 Brazil and Argentina both introduced significant reforms in an attempt to restore order in their economies.

Finally, observation of the success in some developing countries has led to reflection in others about what policies promote growth. This change has been reflected in the deliberative forums of the UN. At a major UNCTAD conference in 1986, and at two special sessions of the UN General Assembly, there has been much greater reference to liberalization and market forces than has been the case in these fora in the past.

Many more developing countries began to liberalize their trade regimes in the early 1980s. By late 1986 the World Bank had extended loans worth US$12 billion to 43 countries. Three-quarters of those programmes were related to domestic plans to liberalize trade restrictions.

The emphasis in the OECD economies through the 1980s to let markets have a bigger say in determining economic activity has also had its reflection among developing countries. The developing countries perceive that they have a major stake in the shape of international trading arrangements and that a more open international trading system of which they too are an integral part is one of the most tangible steps that can be taken to assist their development. Many fewer are sitting back as they were in the 1970s waiting for the industrialized world to deliver growth packages.

Apprehension about the new issues

While two general sets of attitudes towards the trade round have emerged among the developing countries, the differences between them dissipate over the new issues – services, intellectual property and investment. The general attitude is that these are sectors where industries in the industrialized world are strong and that any commitments to new rules will disadvantage the developing countries.

Opposition to an agreement to liberalize services has lessened. A few developing countries have come to see positive benefit in an agreement. Most, however, are apprehensive about how they will be affected. For the majority of developing countries who accept its advent as a reality, the issue is the character of the initial obligations. Most would prefer not to accept binding obligations from the outset because of uncertainty about what the practical effect of the agreement would be over time.

Intellectual property is much more difficult. A number of significant developing countries are opposed to an agreement for the very reason that it is wanted in Washington, Bonn, Berne and Tokyo. Indigenous drug industries have been created to provide cheap, generic drugs to the population. Opposition is rooted in an amalgam of protectionist interests and government social policy. The strongest opposition is from India, Brazil and Egypt. Some of the Asian/Pacific countries are prepared to negotiate to secure some form of multilateral agreement to obviate continuing bilateral US pressure over intellectual property issues. There will be an effort to separate any intellectual property agreement from the formal part of the GATT machinery.

Developing countries are nearly unanimous in their opposition to proposals from the United States and Japan for rules in GATT concerning investment. The proposals are to proscribe the attaching to investment of conditions about trade performance.

Developing countries' bids

While interests among the developing countries are diverse, a common position is that in each new area of agreement provision should be made for 'special and differential' treatment for developing countries. Expectations about what might be agreed at the end of the day vary. More often than not agreement is reached to recognize this provision as a general principle but not to alter the basic obligations substantively.

The strongest application of the principle is supposedly its lightening of the obligation of developing countries to contribute in negotiations to reduce tariffs. However, it is generally accepted that in the Uruguay Round developing countries will participate in the tariff negotiations and reduce and bind tariffs.

The principle has had its clearest enunciation in the agriculture negotiations in which the Cairns Group of agriculture exporters, which mostly comprises developing countries, has suggested that where obligations to liberalize are agreed, developing countries be given more time to adjust to the obligations than industrialized countries.

There is also strong insistence that recognition of the special demands of development should be an integral feature of the services agreement. Some countries would like the agreement written in such a way that the right to take action to foster development would be a fundamental right in the agreement which could override other basic obligations.

The special and differential commitment is bad economics. Analyses of the benefits of liberalization show that unless all countries liberalize at the same time the optimal benefit will not be obtained. Work done by the World Bank demonstrates that in some cases – agriculture is one – if the industrialized countries alone liberalized, there would be a net loss of welfare among the developing countries.

Developing countries strongly support liberalization of textiles and clothing by returning the MFA to the GATT system. They want this done gradually. Some will not benefit by liberalization since they have guaranteed access to markets in industrialized countries, but they are not the most efficient exporters. A commitment to liberalize the MFA will be one of the bottom line positions of the developing countries.

Liberalization of markets for tropical products is a key developing country objective. Modest cuts in tariffs were made by the industrialized countries as part of the Montreal mid-term review. Developing countries seek more cuts as part of the final outcome.

The developing countries are no longer monolithic in the view that liberalization is only an issue for industrialized countries. Many were willing to accept formally, as part of the negotiations, greater GATT obligations in tariff negotiations. They want liberalization of agriculture and textiles and do not want new rules on investment or intellectual property. Virtually all of them will draw the line at suggestions that their rights to use balance of payments grounds for imposing trade barriers be circumscribed. The rule concerned is lax and exploited but it is an issue over which developing countries are solid in opposition.

Chapter Nine
WHO IS CAIRNS?

In October 1987 the Australian Prime Minister, Bob Hawke, was scheduled to address a special meeting at the GATT in Geneva about the importance of the Uruguay Round. A week before, Geneva based delegates of the 13 member Cairns Group of agricultural exporters met to put the finishing touches on a draft of the Group's first comprehensive proposal for liberalization of trade in agriculture. It was to be sent home to capitals for approval.

This was the first time the group had attempted to develop a formal, common set of proposals and this was a further step in the consolidation of the group. To date the group had operated more as a loose coalition than as a common front. The Argentine representative, Nestor Stancanelli, suggested that Hawke announce the proposals in his speech. Other members of the Group were enthusiastic about the idea. Time was tight. In the capitals proposals like this usually had to be cleared by ministers and frequently by more than one. Ministers were always busy and it was never easy to get such clearances quickly.

The Geneva representatives undertook to do what they could. By the eve of the Hawke speaking date all members of the group had received clearances to the proposal from capitals, except one – Brazil. The deputy of the Brazilian delegation in Geneva apologized, but explained that it was impossible to get a decision within the deadline. The relevant ministers and senior officials were not in Brasilia. The head of the foreign ministry, Paulo Tarso Fleche de Lima, was due to return to Brasilia that evening but it would be after office hours.

Hawke was by now in Geneva and his party proposed that the Australian Minister for Trade Negotiations, Michael Duffy, who was also chairman of the Cairns group, try to ring Tarso. Duffy had to be contacted. He was mid-air on a seven hour flight from Singapore to Melbourne. Duffy received a briefing on a stopover at Sydney a few hours later at 6.00 a.m. He could not get through to Tarso but succeeded after arrival in Melbourne two hours later. Tarso was friendly. The two had met three weeks before when Duffy visited Brasilia and had hit it off well.

It was a significant step for Brazil to participate in a group like the Cairns Group because it included developing and industrialized countries. Brazil had traditionally been a strong advocate of developing country solidarity. To keep faith with this it had always insisted that the Cairns Group was 'informal' and that Brazil participated on the basis that the Group was used to coordinate positions rather than agree joint positions. Duffy's request that Brazil agree to the paper so that Hawke could launch it the next day in Geneva meant that Brazil had to address the principle of formal collaboration in the Group with developed countries, and quickly.

There were strong reasons for Brazil to collaborate more formally with the Group and cosponsor the proposal. Of its exports 50 per cent were agricultural. Four important Latin American neighbours were in the Cairns Group and wanted the proposal to proceed. Tarso suggested an understanding. 'Michael, we will support the proposal, but you must give me your assurance that the Cairns Group will support the principle that the special interests of developing countries will be recognized'. 'Paulo, you have my assurance.' Duffy replied. Hawke announced the Cairns Group proposal the following day in Geneva. This action was another step in the evolution of the Cairns Group which had begun early in 1986.

A tough business

The countries in the Cairns Group came together because all were trying to trade in the toughest game in town. Agricultural trade had been a bad business to be in. The terms of trade for primary products and agriculture in particular have declined over the forty years' history of the GATT. Over the last twenty years increasing protection of major markets and subsidization of exports has severely damaged the trade of many exporting nations. The comparative advantage from which efficient producers are supposed to benefit in an open trading system has been denied efficient agricultural exporters. On the other hand trade in manufactures has increased dramatically over the period and terms of trade in manufactures have risen sharply as a result.

A number of countries today face major economic problems which would not have existed had market forces been allowed to dictate production and trade in agriculture to the extent to which market forces shape trade in manufactures. The range of countries affected is surprising and is reflected by the membership of the Cairns Group – Argentina, Brazil, Chile, Colombia and Uruguay from Latin America; Australia, Fiji, Indonesia, Malaysia, New Zealand, the Philippines and Thailand from Asia/Pacific; and Canada and Hungary. (Since Fiji is not a member of GATT, it only participates in the Group when its minsters meet.)

Collectively these Cairns Group companies account for 25 per cent of global trade in agriculture, which supports its claim to represent major interests on a par with the United States and the European Community in international agricultural trade (see Figure 9.1). Within particular commodities, members of the group represent substantial trading interests. Argentina, Australia, Brazil, Canada, and Uruguay account for 50–60 per cent of global exports of beef and veal. New Zealand, Australia, and Argentina account for 80 per cent of mutton and lamb global exports. Argentina, Australia and Canada export 35 per cent of the wheat traded. Argentina, Australia and New Zealand account for 25 per cent of world dairy trade. The Philippines, Australia, Thailand, Fiji, Brazil and Argentina account for 25 per cent of the free global sugar market. Thailand and Australia

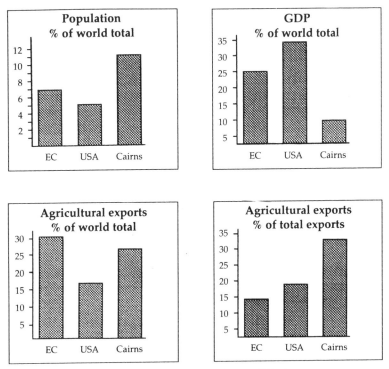

Source: Australian Department of Foreign Affairs and Trade

FIGURE 9.1 *Cairns Group: comparative overview, 1985*

export 35 per cent of the rice exported globally. Chile and Colombia are major horticulture exporters. Malaysia and Brazil are major exporters of vegetable oil and oilseeds.

Australia and New Zealand were major suppliers of agricultural products to the United Kingdom before it joined the European Community. As a member of the Community the United Kingdom could not keep its markets for agricultural products open. As part of its terms of accession, the United Kingdom negotiated for retention of supply of New Zealand butter into the European Community. The New Zealand economy could not have survived without that market. Australia had other agricultural markets and significant minerals exports and it was not so critically dependent on the EC market.

Europe is the main market for beef exported from Argentina, Uruguay and Brazil. The market has shrunk dramatically over the years, particularly over the last decade as heavy subsidization has shifted the European Community from being a major importer to major exporter of beef. If Argentina exported today what it used to export its debt burden would be completely manageable. If any country in the world has a natural advantage for production of agricultural products, especially grain and cereals, it is Argentina. The situation is almost the same for Uruguay. It is heavily dependent on exports of beef and its economy has stagnated as its market shrank.

In absolute terms Brazil is a huge exporter. Brazil is less dependent on agricultural exports than its Latin American neighbours, but 50 per cent of its exports are still agriculture. It is a very large beef producer and as well a significant exporter of soya beans and chicken. Other Latin American countries are also major agricultural exporters. Colombia is better known for its coffee. But it is a significant exporter of horticultural products to the European Community and the United States, especially cut flowers. Chile's exports are mainly fruit and vegetables to the same market.

Fluctuations in the world sugar markets as a result of protection in the United States and the Community has badly affected the Philippines for which sugar has been a major export. From the early to the mid 1980s, the markets were so bad that exports from the Philippines fell by 90 per cent. There were severe economic problems in one of the provinces which was a major sugar producing area. The depression of the sugar market also affected exports from Australia, Thailand, Argentina, Fiji and Brazil. Malaysia is a major producer of many commodities of which palm oil is potentially most threatened by overproduction of oils and fats on the global market as a result of subsidization.

Thailand is one of the world's largest rice exporters. The major markets which it should be able to supply – the European Community and Japan – are closed. Indonesia is also a major commodity exporter. Among agricultural products, rice is the one with the greatest interest. Over the years Indonesia has shifted from being a major exporter to a major importer. As rice production increases Indonesia may return to exporting.

Hungary is the most efficient agricultural exporter in Europe. It has had significant veal exports into the Community, but these have been restricted over the years. Until the opening up of Eastern Europe Hungary faced a perpetual threat from the Community – either closure of markets or being undercut with cheap products. Canada has major western plain agricultural export interests in beef and wheat. Its export markets in wheat were particularly affected by the subsidy war between the United States and the European Community. On the east coast however, Canada's agriculture is heavily protected and entrenched. The major product is dairy.

The European Community the United States and Japan are major markets for the products of the Cairns exporters. In every one of these markets there are major restrictions and barriers. The United States and the European Community are also major exporters and hold significant shares of trade through the use of subsidies. Nearly every product exported from the Community and grain exports from the United States are subsidized. While the use of subsidies to promote the export of manufactures was disallowed in the GATT in the early 1960s, the right to subsidize exports of primary products was left unchanged.

For all of these countries there is a direct relationship between the level of their agricultural exports and economic growth. It is so important for a number of them that they could walk away from the international trade negotiations if liberalization of trade in agriculture does not begin. Five of the Cairns countries are among the IMF list of most heavily indebted countries. Both Australia and New Zealand are unilaterally liberalizing their manufacturing sectors. They can do without GATT if they want. The Round would have very limited value to their economies if agricultural markets were not liberalized.

Second class status

The efficient agricultural exporters have watched powerlessly over the years as agriculture's second class status in GATT developed. A steady series of exceptions to the GATT rules of trade in agriculture developed. The first was small. The original GATT rules prohibited the use of quotas to restrain imports other than for remedial action in specific, approved circumstances. But there was one exception: where programmes existed ostensibly to restrain agricultural production, import quotas were allowed. In 1955 the United States secured formal approval ('a waiver' in GATT law) to exempt from GATT rules parts of its agricultural production. In the early 1960s subsidization of exports by governments was banned in GATT, except for primary products. In 1966 Switzerland negotiated its entry to GATT on condition that its agricultural sector was exempt from GATT rules. And when EC expenditure on the CAP started to rise from the mid-1970s as the Community made the transition from agricultural importer to exporter, its representatives made it clear that GATT rules were not relevant to the CAP.

The period from the mid-1970s on was particularly inhospitable for efficient agricultural exporters. The European Community overproduced, depressing prices, stealing some markets and threatening nearly all markets with its overhanging surpluses. The United States increased the protection of its domestic market for some products; but even worse it financed a war chest to recapture its markets from the European Community. The programmes also enabled the United States to dispose of excess stocks.

In the GATT the European Community as a matter of course for several years blocked any systematic discussion of problems in agricultural trade. The GATT dispute settlement system was not allowed to function where cases involving agriculture were submitted to it. First the Community and then the United States would not accept findings unfavourable to them. At the disastrous GATT ministerial meeting in 1982 the United States and the European Community negotiated between themselves over how agriculture might be handled in GATT in future. The United States, which wanted progress, found that the Community did not want to negotiate seriously. The agreement which was negotiated was weak. The Australians regarded it as meaningless and, in melodramatic display, walked out of the meeting.

The efficient exporters all shared the conviction of being hard done by the big three and the small Europeans outside the Economic Community who hid behind their protectionist skirts. They faced the frustration of being the best in the business – cheapest and best quality – and seeing the markets rigged. Some were facing declines in the standard of living of their people. Trade officials from these countries were used to collaborating with each other. All were members of commodity arrangements or informal groups where they were accustomed to swapping notes and even cooperating in markets on occasions. The common interest was strong and possibility of collaboration was obvious.

Cairns

In 1985 John Dawkins was made Trade Minister in the reform minded Australian Labor government which had been elected two years before. He shook his sleepy administration and offered the author the job as Australia's GATT ambassador in Geneva. At the end of 1985 the author returned and reviewed the situation with Dawkins. A new trade round was on the cards. To ensure that agriculture was a central part of it a more powerful expression of the interests of the efficient exporters had to be achieved. A coalition of interests was needed. Matters should not be left in the hands of the European Community and the United States as they had been in the past. To test the interest Dawkins planned to invite the trade ministers of the disadvantaged agricultural exporters to a meeting in Australia to discuss agricultural reform.

Collaboration was canvassed in Geneva among the Australians, Uruguayans and New Zealanders. In March 1986 the Uruguayans invited officials from Argentina, Australia, Brazil and New Zealand to a meeting in Montevideo to discuss agricultural trade reform. The idea of the wider group was canvassed. The Australians had separately discussed this with the Thais who hosted a meeting of a wider group of officials in Pattaya in July. This became a preliminary meeting to a meeting of ministers which Dawkins would host in August just before the Punta meeting.

Cairns is the small resort town in tropical Northern Australia from which most tourists visit the Great Barrier Reef, the largest natural coral reef in the world. It is the centre of Australia's sugar producing area. Dawkins thought that holding the meeting in Cairns might also give the local branch of the Labor Party something of a fillip. A regional election was imminent. That interest was not satisfied at all – the local Labor Party did not succeed. But the meeting did.

The European Community gave them something extra to sink their teeth into. Two weeks before in Geneva, at the final meeting of the committee which had been set up a year before to prepare for the ministerial meeting at Punta, the French blocked endorsement by EC member states of the draft declaration for Punta. This had been prepared by officials in Geneva and the Community had helped negotiate the text. The French would not let the Community endorse it, even as a negotiating text, because they considered that it committed the Community to negotiating to liberalize agriculture.

At Cairns the ministers agreed they should work collectively at the Punta meeting three weeks later. They would try to improve the proposals for the negotiations that the French thought went too far. This was the first time in GATT's modern history that a group of countries drawn from the ranks of developing countries, industrialized countries and Eastern Europe had collaborated to advance common positions.

The group succeeded for four reasons. First, its common interests were strong. Every country in the group saw significant, identifiable benefits in increased export earnings if agricultural markets were opened. The strength of the interest was in direct proportion to the levels of protection in the major markets. Second, the primary level of commitment in the group was at ministerial level. Third, the group satisfied domestic political needs of its members. The year it formed saw agricultural prices sink to recent record lows: a full-scale subsidy war between the United States and the European Community broke out; and nearly every agricultural and trade minister in a Cairns country was under pressure. The Cairns Group showed they were acting. Fourth, agricultural trade was the major trade problem between the United States and the European Community. Cairns agitation amplified the dimension of the issue.

The agriculture crisis

1987 showed that there was a serious need to bring agriculture within the orbit of GATT rules. As well as the damage being done to other exporters like the Cairns countries, the terms upon which countries can trade in agricultural products became a major source of dispute, yet again between the United States and the European Community. The issue had been a running sore between the two since the mid–1970s.

The year began with the culmination of the biggest US–EC trade dispute yet. The issue was the terms upon which Spain and Portugal joined the Community. Under GATT rules parties which want to form customs unions and replace national tariffs with a common tariff are obliged to show that the net result would not lead to a rise in trade barriers. The Community treated its GATT obligations offhandedly. Other GATT parties were consulted in 1986 only after the Community had completed internal negotiations. There was little scope for changing them. The United States reckoned that the net result of the changes was that it would lose about US$500 million agricultural exports to the Community. The latter in turn contended that the United States would regain this trade in other areas because of the overall improvement in access to the markets of Spain and Portugal for industrial products.

After a long series of protracted negotiations the United States informed the Community in late 1986 that on 31 January 1987 it would retaliate under the provisions of Section 301 of its domestic trade law and raise tariffs to the value of half a billion dollars on EC exports to the United States. The list included French cognac, British whisky and German luxury automobiles. The Community settled under duress. It did not believe that the US case was watertight but its member states were not prepared to enter a drawn out trade war. The atmosphere between US and EC officials was bitter.

The US–EC subsidy war intensified. The US agriculture industry contended that progressive increases in subsidies by the Community in recent years had enabled it to increase its share of markets. Congress had created the export enhancement programme to subsidize US farmers back into these markets. Cairns Group exporters were horrified. They could not finance their farmers to compete with the United States and the European Community. In 1987 they battened down and watched world prices drop and saw their export receipts diminish as the United States and the European Community competed for markets with lower and lower prices. Many of them faced significant domestic unrest from their farmers.

The Community and United States both accepted that this had gone too far, although they both kept subsidizing and accusing the other of compounding the problem. Andriessen was working to reform the CAP to reduce costs. Yeutter was committed to the Uruguay Round and wanted to see it used to liberalize agricultural trade. In June 1987 at the annual economic summit of the seven major economic powers in Venice the issue of reform of agricultural trade was on the agenda for the first time. Canada put the point of view of the Cairns Group countries. The leaders committed their governments to put major negotiating proposals on the table in Geneva in the trade round negotiations by the end of the year. The importance of negotiating agreements on agriculture in the Round was underlined. No other trade issue in the Round was signalled out for this attention.

The Cairns' goals

The Cairns Group put detailed proposals on the table at every juncture of the negotiations. Philosophically, they stand close to the US positions. The United States put proposals forward for complete liberalization. So did the Cairns Group. Their ultimate goal was to see market forces dictate production and trade of agriculture. As efficient producers they would benefit handsomely. They know that this has to be a long-term goal given how entrenched protection is in the United States, the European Community and Japan.

They have several specific short-term objectives to satisfy. They want greater access granted to markets. Some markets, particularly in the European Community, are almost completely closed. They are very concerned that reform is reflected in new rules, particularly the phase out of the right to use export subsidies. While an agreement to reduce the amount of money spent on export subsidies would be welcome, it is no substitute for agreement to a permanent change to the rule which permits the subsidies. For so long as subsidization is permitted it is open at any time to someone to increase the level of funding for agricultural protection. This is fundamental for Cairns countries. They can never aspire to match the level of subsidies that the 'big three' can afford without bankrupting their treasuries and ruining their agricultural sectors.

The Group articulated careful proposals about how the interests of developing countries might be recognized. The Group did not want to depart from free trade principles in its proposals for liberalization. They also wanted to avoid agreeing in principle to exceptions of principle. These had characterized the protectionism of Europeans for years. The Europeans had always argued that agriculture had 'special characteristics' which meant that ordinary economics and rules of trade could not apply. The Cairns countries tended to find that the solution lay in providing developing countries with longer periods of time to implement reform than industrialized countries.

They also had sympathy for the potential problem of the net food importing developing countries. Some of the arguments about problems caused by increased food import bills if liberalization raised food prices were overstated. Liberalization would not be rapid. There was also a degree of exploitation of these concerns by developing countries who were members of the Lomé convention, as a means of putting pressure on the Community not to cut Lomé benefits. Cairns countries emphasized the importance of special assistance from the World Bank to assist net food developing country importers to deal with any changes that liberalization might bring about.

The Cairns Group has evinced a better understanding of what determines EC positions than the United States has. It therefore tended to recognize this more in its proposals than the US would, but not to the extent that it moved away from the liberal trade basis of the approach of the US. Because of this, the Group was able to frame proposals in a way that assisted the process of negotiation.

The Group was to make several contributions to the negotiations. Demonstrating the efficacy of collaboration across group lines had a most beneficial effect on the negotiations across the board. A number of other joint proposals in other areas of the negotiations from other groupings of countries were developed.

In the agriculture negotiations themselves the Group's approach on reform of rules has kept this issue central in the negotiations. Its careful approach to the process of negotiations has assisted the chairman of the negotiating group and others to devise approaches to keep the negotiations moving forward, particularly in face of impasses between the United States and the European Community. Finally, crystallization of the importance of the issues in the minds of individual members of the group and the militancy which the Latin American members of the Group brought to the negotiations is what kept the basic compact between the new issues and the old issues in place. This compact was the driving force of the Round.

As far as most members of the Cairns Group were concerned the Round and the multilateral trading system were not worth having without agricultural trade liberalization. This is a reflection of their self-interest.

But given that protection of agriculture has been the greatest departure by the United States, the European Community and Japan from the GATT multilateral trading system, given that liberalization of trade in agriculture is directly linked to efforts to solve the Latin American debt problem and to stimulate development, given that moving agriculture into GATT will lay the basis for reducing US–EC trade wars, given the enormous gains in net welfare to be enjoyed by industrialized and developing countries, there is a significant degree of objectivity in the Cairns' perspective.

Part Three

THE
NEGOTIATIONS

INTRODUCTION – WHAT IS GATT?

An easy target

Lester Thurow, the American economist who knows the publicity value of a good line, won international coverage at the annual international businessmen's talk and ski convention at Davos, Switzerland in 1988 for declaring that 'GATT is dead'. This was not exactly what he said but this was how the media, who along with the businessmen and free trade economists loved it, reported it. GATT has always had tough publicity. It is an easy target.

Businessmen are sceptical because it is slow moving – either not eliminating trade barriers quickly, or not quickly giving protection against an import which is damaging their business – and because its operations are obscured by dense, bureaucratic language and complicated concepts. GATT sets international competition laws. Businesses that are competitive like it because GATT rules encourage fair price competition. Business that is not competitive feels threatened by GATT rules.

GATT is frequently the foil in arguments between business and government over protective measures. Its rules are invoked by officials as grounds for not meeting demands from business for protection; its ineffectiveness is emphasized by business when arguing for protection. Sensing the scepticism of their readers, journalists focus on the disproportion between great effort and modest result in the trade negotiations – few achievements pass this test.

The toughest critics are its allies – the fraternity of liberal economists. Free trade is the closest thing to religion for many liberal economists and they are therefore inclined to judge harshly if their institutional progeny errs. The standards which are set for it are tough. The most effective criticism of GATT is that it is a hollow vessel. It is argued that so much trade is conducted outside its rules that it does not work. GATT has been made less effective by the major trading powers since the mid-1970s because they have removed a significant proportion of world trade from GATT rules.

Some economists have gone so far as to suggest that only 7 per cent of world trade is covered by GATT. The conventional figure is 50 per cent. Neither can be satisfactorily demonstrated, but it is undeniable that a very substantial proportion of world trade is not conducted under the GATT rules of international competition. But there has never been a time when the system of international trade laid down by the GATT rules did not have major dead spots – significant areas of trade in which the GATT rules were not applied.

Notwithstanding this shortcoming, the GATT remains a valuable instrument. Its basic principles are respected more than breached and remain the yardstick for the conduct of international trade. Multilateral trade laws based on liberal principles with flaws are better than none at all. If the GATT did not exist today, it would have to be invented.

The most simplistic critics are the media: not the informed handful who cover international trade but the news journalists and commentators sent to cover an important meeting. Often they find that what is happening is not newsworthy in that it is not worth a catchy headline. In a commendable effort to reduce what they are covering to something comprehensible for their readers or viewers, they address fundamental issues – if nothing is happening, will this lead to the formation of trade blocs or will this cause an outbreak of a trade war? The story then is not the GATT meeting but a trade bloc or trade war story.

GATT – a two-part process

GATT is an international treaty. It is difficult to read, not only because lawyers helped to draft it but also because a lot of its provisions were compromises. When countries accede to the Agreement they adopt a set of international laws governing how they regulate trade. They do not commit themselves immediately to removing all trade barriers but to supporting open markets and market forces.

To paraphrase Professor Hudec at the University of Minnesota, one of the most lucid students of GATT, the key obligations of the Agreement are:

1. To use only approved instruments of protection, primarily the tariff.

2. To use the instruments in a non-discriminatory way, extending any opening of a market to all GATT trading partners.

3. To submit all protection to a long-term process on non-reversible reductions through negotiations.

Once the Agreement came into force in the late 1940s, it evolved fairly quickly into a two-part process. The first part is the day to day work of policing and refining the rules of the General Agreement. The principal rules are set out in Appendix 3. A key part of this are the dispute procedures where one party can ask for adjudication over a breach of rights by another party. This would usually be a measure to restrict imports which the complaining party considered in breach of GATT rules.

The GATT council meets every six weeks or so in Geneva. Its primary business is to administer the disputes system. It is also the management committee of GATT. Various administrative and policy bodies established report to it.

The second part of the process are the major conferences which are convened every few years for the sole purpose of negotiating to reduce tariffs and other barriers to open markets. These became known as the 'Rounds' of trade negotiations. The Uruguay Round is the eighth.

An evolving process

Whereas the first trade rounds forty years ago were devoted almost entirely to negotiations to lower tariffs, the scope has become much wider. The purpose of rounds has extended to include the drafting of new rules which reduce trade barriers and open trade but are not negotiated in the way specific reductions to tariffs are negotiated. The inclusion of new issues, particularly services, has fundamentally altered the character and scope of the Uruguay Round negotiation compared to rounds in the past. The measures of success will also be different. The Uruguay Round cannot be divorced from contemporary events. The other measure of its success is the relevance of its outcomes to the consequences of those events.

Chapter Ten
THE ROAD TO PUNTA DEL ESTE

In the third week of September 1986 the casino at the main hotel at Punta del Este was treated to its most distinguished clientele since the meeting of presidents of the American republics nearly twenty years before. Ministers, grey-suited officials and suave diplomats from Geneva crowded into a makeshift conference room to hear incomprehensible reports about documents and consultations. This was the sort of thing that was the stuff of life in the conference halls in Geneva but made little sense outside.

One of the endearing qualities of GATT meetings is that long speeches are discouraged. The other is that by the distorted standards of international diplomacy debate is rather direct. The meeting in Punta was scheduled for three and a half days. UN meetings of this magnitude would run for six weeks and usually achieve less.

Within 48 hours the ministers would be locked into a process which had to produce a result. Those who went to Punta were ready for a result, although it was not apparent to most of them at the time. Ministers arrived at Punta with two major issues, and some other sticky ones, unresolved. It had been hard work getting even that far.

International trade negotiations are like complicated, voluntary mergers of very large public companies. To make them work a certain amount of luck is involved. There needs to be the right chemistry between the boards and the chief executives. Major shareholder interests have to be satisfied. The financial interests of the companies have to be compatible, finance at the right price may need to be available and the economic climate has to be right. They usually take a long time to set up. In short, the stars have to be aligned.

The beginnings of the Uruguay Round were auspicious. There was satisfactory growth in the international economy. There were enough governments who wanted it badly enough. It was launched at a time of crisis in international agricultural markets and a period of historic modernization of the character of international trade. It was launched by politicians committed to strengthening international market mechanisms and it has occurred during one of the great realignments of political and economic power in the history of Europe. Its success or otherwise was to be entirely a function of those in power.

The push for Punta

In mid 1985 the Americans decided that it was time to start to pushing to get a decision to launch a trade round. They needed a firm commitment from the European Community and a decision in GATT to proceed. The Swedish government had hosted an informal meeting of trade ministers in June. Discussions among the ministers proceeded on the premise that there were no objections to the convening of a round. More encouraging, there was even a very productive discussion on the thorny issue of how services would be handled.

The ministers present from Brazil and India were much more constructive than their officials had been in similar discussions in Geneva and the communiqué from the meetings appeared to carry an endorsement of the idea of a round and the concept that services could be included in the negotiations provided negotiations on them were conducted separately from negotiations on goods – parallel but separate was the slogan.

Everybody left Stockholm in a buoyant mood. A trade round seemed in their grasp. A decision was still needed in GATT to set dates and prepare the ground and it was here that what appeared to have been agreed among Ministers was unpicked. Brazil's ambassador to GATT was Paulo Batista. Batista was a man of Brazilian charm and entrepreneurial manner. He smoked Cuban cigars and liked to work in shirtsleeves and braces. He was a diplomat's attorney and loved pleading cases and the intricacies of drafting – he was ever ready to reach for a freshly sharpened pencil and relished being in the thick of things.

Back in Geneva the Brazilians let it be known widely (directly in private, more obliquely in public) that the position adopted by the Brazilian minister in Stockholm had to be 'understood'. In diplomatic parlance this meant that the Brazilians would continue to be as intransigent as ever and that events in Stockholm would be ignored. A Latin American from a neighbour of Brazil opined that Brazil's foreign ministry careerists would have been mortified at how forthcoming their minister had been. It was far too soon to have given such ground.

The Americans reviewed their options. It was clear that India and Brazil would continue to procrastinate and delay a decision. The traditional means of taking a decision in GATT was by consensus. There were enough other developing countries with reservations about services to support Brazil for only a forced vote to yield a decision. The Americans decided to request a postal ballot among GATT contracting parties that a special session of the contracting parties be convened to set up a preparatory committee for a round of international trade negotiations.

They checked privately and established that the chances of getting the necessary two-thirds majority were good. Japan, the European Community, the non-EC Europeans, the Pacific rim countries and the Latin agricultural exporters all told the United States privately that they would vote yes in the ballot. The returns came in over the European summer break and confirmed that this assessment was correct. The special session of the contracting parties was convened.

It was clear before the meeting was held that the numbers were there to secure the decision. No one was going to press for a vote simply to demonstrate that they could be voted down. As the meeting drew to a conclusion, the Community unexpectedly found itself in difficulty. The French did not have instructions that permitted them to support the setting up of a preparatory committee. The entire meeting was held up while the Community went into a huddle on the conference room floor. There were hurried consultations and telephone calls to Paris. In the end the French acquiesced. This would not be the first time that the French would hold the Community up because of ambivalence about the round.

The decision was taken to establish a preparatory committee for a new round of international trade negotiations. Arthur Dunkel, the Director-General of GATT, was appointed chairman of the preparatory committee.

To the observer off the street, the September decision was effectively a decision to convene a trade round. But the trade officials knew that there was a lot that had to be done to get a trade round started properly. It was essential that a well developed set of objectives for the negotiations be prepared for ministers to consider. It was not enough simply to get the ministers together. The disaster of the GATT ministerial meeting of 1982 could not be repeated. It soon became clear that those who were not committed to a trade round intended to continue to impede progress.

Taking matters into their own hands

Arthur Dunkel was Swiss by nationality, but always went to pains to stress that in his job the only nationality he carried was GATT's. An elegant dresser, Dunkel was a gracious man nearly permanently enveloped in clouds of Gitane smoke. Before his appointment as Director-General in 1980 he had been a senior Swiss trade negotiator.

Dunkel was faced with a delicate situation. The Americans and their supporters wanted to get on with the job. They had been impatient with the stalling to date. The Americans were threatening publicly that unless the GATT process could be proved effective they would give up on it and focus their attention on their alternative concept of setting up a network of free trade areas. It was known that they had had discussions at various levels with Israel, Canada and the ASEAN countries.

On the other hand the Indians and the Brazilians and their

supporters had warned Dunkel that the tactics of confrontation were counter-productive. They argued that the calling of the vote to set up the preparatory committee had been a divisive tactic which went against the GATT tradition of decision by consensus. Dunkel was also receiving regular counsel from Tran, the EC ambassador, that he had to keep GATT a united house.

Dunkel convened a series of committee meetings in late 1985 and early 1986. Various delegations introduced papers on particular subjects with drafts of proposals for the negotiations. For meeting after meeting there were arid exchanges. India and Brazil, supported at various times by Egypt, Tanzania, Cuba and Yugoslavia, made long legalistic interventions about the inappropriateness of including services in the negotiations. They focused as well on some other new issues which the Americans wanted included – establishment of trade rights to deal with intellectual property infringements, and restrictions on investment measures which distorted trade. These were points of view which all developing countries, including those who wanted a trade round, shared.

Dunkel was evidently stuck. He knew that there was no point in trying to pull a small group together to start to find common ground. No signals of preparedness to do so were being given by the foot draggers. In the meantime he concentrated on securing agreement to the date of the ministerial conference and the location. The location was the more sensitive issue. Where a conference was held affected national prestige. The Uruguayans and the Canadians made direct offers. The European Community expressed an informal interest.

Following discussions among the Swiss, Swedish, Canadian, Australian and New Zealand Ambassadors, these five met with their colleagues from Finland, Norway, Austria and Iceland and began the task of compiling a draft of a set of objectives for the trade round to go before the ministers. They developed a very rough paper drawing on the various texts on individual issues that delegations had put on the table in Dunkel's preparatory committee.

They then approached several ambassadors from among the developing countries which were keen to see the round launched. Foremost among these were Felipe Jaramillo, Colombia's representative to the GATT, and Julio Lacarte-Muro, the doyen of the GATT fraternity. Lacarte had been at the original Havana conference in 1946/8 from which GATT had emerged. The Australians and the New Zealanders raised the matter with the Aseans and South Koreans. For several months these countries, with Japan, had met regularly over lunch to discuss GATT issues. Officials from these nine countries had been meeting occasionally in capitals to discuss international trade issues since 1984.

The developing countries which had been approached then met among themselves, agreed to open a dialogue with the small industrialized countries and dubbed themselves the Group of 20. These two groups met twice. It was the common view that action was necessary to get a draft declaration ready. There was concern, however, that there was little point in members of that group negotiating among themselves. It was with the big three that the deals had to be struck.

A couple of evenings later the Korean Ambassador, Kun Park, hosted a dinner for a select group of senior officials from capitals and for Geneva ambassadors. The foot draggers were not present. There was great interest in the dialogue between the 9 and the 20. Pierre Louis Girard, the Swiss ambassador to GATT who used to describe himself as a working-class boy from the Valais and who had an unerring capacity to go straight to the point, challenged the Americans, the European Community and the Japanese to join the 9 and the 20 and forge ahead and negotiate a negotiating set of objectives for the ministers to consider. He reflected a widely held sentiment that Brazil and India were not interested in seeing a successful trade round; and that if everyone continued to wait for a result from Dunkel's preparatory committee the round might be doomed.

Everybody knew that there were at least a dozen different areas in which negotiating objectives had to be prepared. Some of these were very difficult subjects and would themselves require substantial negotiation among officials. Experienced negotiators understood that it was essential not to overload the agenda for the ministers. The objective would be to reduce to a minimum the areas of disagreement and, in the difficult subject areas, to reduce to a minimum the number of unresolved issues.

Contrary to the public image, successful negotiations on

complex subjects do not depend on the cleverness of individual negotiators at the eleventh hour in the smoke filled backroom. A prerequisite for success is the many hours of private preparatory discussions among negotiators in which they engage constructively. The parameters of the negotiations are agreed, then agreement on the peripherals is progressively achieved, the number of outstanding issues is whittled down and finally the remaining unresolved issues are left standing. In a successful process these will be the most difficult political issues.

Girard's final point was that time was running out. Dunkel had settled a date for the ministerial meeting – the third week in September. Preparatory work had to conclude at the end of July to give the GATT secretariat time to edit, translate and publish all the documents for the meeting. Mike Smith, Yeutter's deputy from Washington was present and as bullish as ever. The big three agreed that it was time to act. They would begin to negotiate with the 9 and the 20.

GATT goes to EFTA

The view from the expensive Geneva suburb of Cologny across Lake Léman is of the world's largest conference complex. The former League of Nations headquarters (now the UN's European headquarters) sits in the middle. It is surrounded by seven large and many smaller organizations each with their own, usually plush headquarters building. The area is like a permanent Expo site for government officials.

About a kilometre and a half from GATT's lakeside headquarters is the headquarters of EFTA (the European Free Trade Association, of which Sweden, Norway, Iceland, Finland, Austria and Switzerland are members). The building has two intermediate and several smaller conference rooms. It also houses the offices of the delegations to GATT of several of the EFTA countries.

On 20 July 1968, representatives of over 40 GATT delegations gathered in one of the larger conference rooms in the EFTA building. In an unprecedented act of unorthodoxy they had decamped from the GATT building to begin their own process of drafting a negotiating set of objectives for the trade round.

The process ground on for ten days, over weekends and long into every night. For the final few nights the negotiators averaged only three to five hours sleep. As they got more tired and the issues got harder tempers frayed. They worked their way through the dozen or so issues that had been identified as the major subjects for the negotiations. The hard issues were left to last.

The big issues

The discussions on services were wary. The developing countries present were aware that they were in a tricky position. Their negotiating hand was weaker than it would have been had India and Brazil been present. Led by the Singaporean ambassador, Chew Tai Soo, they insisted that the big three undertake that they would hold to whatever was negotiated in the EFTA building. This was agreed.

A consensus was achieved on services in which it was basically agreed that efforts would not be made to link the offer of concessions in the goods area to demands for concessions in the services area. It would be twelve months before anybody had a clear idea of how the negotiations to liberalize services might work. But developing countries appreciated that services trade was dominated by the major trading countries and that services sectors in developing economies were on the whole immature. Their suspicion was that they would lose if there was linkage. They were the demandeurs for access to the goods markets of the industrialized countries. They all knew as well that this was going to be one of the most controversial subjects among the ministers.

The last issue to be addressed in the EFTA process foreshadowed the central importance it was to come to play in the Uruguay Round – agriculture. During discussions in the Dunkel preparatory committee six countries submitted a common paper on objectives for the agricultural negotiations. They were Australia, Chile, Colombia, Thailand, New Zealand and Uruguay. Argentina had been invited to join but chose to submit its own paper. At that point as well Argentina was in company with Brazil and India. In the background the countries which were ultimately to come together as the Cairns Group were starting to coalesce. A meeting of capital based officials in Pattaya, Thailand was set.

By common consent agriculture had been kept as the last subject to be dealt with in the EFTA discussions. Despite the fact that Argentina had not been invited generally to participate in the EFTA negotiations, it was invited to join them over what the objective of the agriculture negotiations should be.

The day before the EFTA process ended the Thai delegation received the text of the communiqué from the meeting of capital based officials in Pattaya. They were to hold out for objectives which promised real change. The Australians had been instructed not to allow the chance for ministers to address this issue properly to be negotiated away. At the beginning of the last day of negotiations the Argentine ambassador, Leopoldo Tettamanti, approached the Australian ambassador. 'If your instructions are to achieve commitment to negotiations for real reform, I am with you to the end.'

This was not histrionics, as Tettamanti showed on more than one occasion. The negotiations were between the European Community supported by the EFTA countries led by Finland, Australia, supported by the Argentines, Uruguayans, Chileans, New Zealanders, Canadians and Thais, and the Americans. They dragged on until three in the morning. The Australians wanted to keep a reference to the possibility of eliminating export subsidies in the text to go to ministers. They wanted the subject referred to where the document dealt with subsidies and where it dealt with agriculture.

The Community would not accept either. Tran was being closely tagged by the French. The European Commission always insists that only the EC member state which is the current president of the European Council may accompany its negotiators to the negotiating table. The French were not allowed into the room but every time Tran stepped outside he was tackled by them. They were adamant that the EC should not commit itself to negotiating reductions in protection of agriculture.

There was a deadlock. Girard and Jaramillo, who had been chairing the meeting, told every one to go home. They retired to Girard's office, invited Tim Groser, the deputy in the New Zealand mission to join them, opened a bottle of scotch and reflected. They wanted a text without brackets. This always minimized the chance of issues being re-opened. They would create a clean text. This would be the chairman's text. People could take it or leave it. The trick was to get it right so that no one could reasonably reject it. They split the difference between the position of the European Community and the Australians and the others. There would be no reference to the possibility of eliminating export subsidies but the issue of subsidies would appear twice, contrary to the Community's wishes.

The group reconvened a few hours later to consider the chairman's text. Some dubbed it the *café au lait* text in deference to famous Colombian/ Swiss products. It was a good result, although the Australians and their colleagues 'reserved' on the agriculture section. This meant that they were not bound by what was contained in it and did not have to take it as a starting point when ministers began to consider the text at Punta. They were careful to indicate, however, that they supported the rest of the text.

At the final meeting of the preparatory committee, the text was introduced on behalf of the 47 countries which had participated in the process in the EFTA building. India and Brazil introduced a much shorter and more limited text on behalf of 10 countries. It was clear where the mainstream opinion lay. The determination of those countries who wanted the trade round launched was also clear. They would not be held up again. But the final sensation was yet to come.

The European Community announced that it could not support the text of the Group of 47. The reason was that the French considered that the section on agriculture went too far and would not allow the Community to endorse the entire document. The Community did not have time to go into its usual elaborate process of internal consultation by which it resolves such differences and had no choice but to abstain. This gave the Americans and others a field day with the media, who by now had observed a persistent pattern of EC uncertainty about whether or not it wanted trade liberalization.

The Punta declaration

The Uruguay Round might have been the Canada Round if the Canadians had offered Vancouver instead of Montreal and tuned in more acutely to the new Pacific influence among the forces pushing for the trade round. The Uruguayans were a strong sentimental candidate. There was strength in the argument that it was time to launch a trade round in a developing country. Their foreign minister, Enrique Iglesias, was internationally popular and competent. He had considerable charm. His president described him as having the capacity to sell refrigerators to Eskimos. Their ambassador to the GATT, Julio Lacarte, was GATT's mentor. The pair obviously had a stake in the favourable publicity that hosting such a meeting would generate for Uruguay, particularly given the bruising its international reputation had taken while it had been under military rule. The deal in the end was that the round would be launched in Uruguay, a mid-term review would be held in Montreal and the Community held the option to host the closing session.

The Group of 47 had done its work well. Most of what it had negotiated would be accepted by the ministers without comment. This meant there would be separate negotiations in the Round to:

1. Reduce tariffs.
2. Circumscribe non-tariff measures.
3. Improve safeguards (emergency protection) arrangements.
4. Control better the incidence of subsidies.
5. Improve the institutional structure of the GATT.
6. Improve the dispute settlement procedures.
7. Consider ending the special protective arrangements governing trade in textiles.
8. Improve access for tropical products.
9. Reduce barriers to trade in natural resource based products.
10. Improve the codes which set special rules on various facets of trade.

Following the pattern in the negotiations among the officials in Geneva, most of the negotiating time at the conference was spent on one 'old' issue – agriculture – and three 'new' ones – services, intellectual property and investment measures related to trade.

Discussion of textiles was limited. The statement of purpose of the textile negotiations in the Group of 47's paper was very weak. This was deliberate. Negotiations on this had been led by Hong Kong and Korea. The US textile lobby in the US Congress was in a dangerous mood. They did not want anything to happen in GATT. Since a new version of the MFA had been negotiated in Geneva just over a month before, the leading textile exporters decided that they would not press too hard at that stage. It was an issue for later in the round.

The Community was in the spotlight over agriculture, having been forced by the French to reserve in Geneva just over a month before on the entire Group of 47 draft declaration. The French trade minister, the handsome champion oarsman Michel Noir, was to be joined by the nuggety French agriculture minister and former farmers' union leader François Guillaume. This led to much speculation, especially among the EC delegations. Was Guillaume coming to shore up or restrict Noir? The experienced Paris watchers regarded Guillaume's presence as a good sign. He was more senior than Noir and it meant new ground could be broken if necessary.

In the foyer outside the main conference room, there were official notice boards announcing what meetings were being held in what room. Geneva diplomats develop fixed habits over time. One is to hold meetings of this group or that group, even if no purpose is to be served. The point seems to be that if there is an international conference, then, as a matter of course all the groups meet. As a result the notice boards are watched.

As delegates entered this foyer area the day before the meeting began to register and familiarize themselves with the surroundings they saw an unfamiliar entry on the notice board. 'Meeting of Cairns Group—Room III, 1500.' At Cairns the ministers had agreed to cooperate at Punta del Este to get the best possible deal on agriculture.

US officials basically thought that the Group of 47's language on agriculture – which had been objected to by both the

Community and the key Cairns Group countries – was not too bad. It had some gobbledygook but given that this was a subject that had not been discussed seriously in GATT in years this represented an agreement to negotiate. Why not force the Community and everyone else to go along with what was there?

But Dick Lyng, the US Secretary for Agriculture, who was negotiating for the United States did not like the negativeness of the Community. And when he saw the preparedness of this new, peculiar coalition of ministers who had determined a month before to get a better result, he decided that the United States should join them. Clayton Yeutter agreed.

Some EC officials had difficulty adjusting to the idea of the Community having to negotiate with the United States as well as this 'Cairns Group'. After the first meeting betwen the Cairns Group and the Community at which initial positions were exchanged, one senior EC official, who was to retire shortly after the Punta meeting made a point of remarking to the Thai representatives as they left that they should not be under any illusion that their representations were going to have any effect.

The point at issue in the negotiations was whether or not the objective of the negotiations was to be liberalization of agricultural trade or re-regulation of it. The United States and the Cairns Group wanted a clear statement that the objective of the negotiations should be liberalization. The European Community wanted the emphasis to be on regulating agricultural markets. Liberalization was still not on its agenda.

The difference was resolved by amending the proposal in the draft prepared by the 47. The United States and the Cairns Group considered that the European Community had moved towards their position. The Community was content that it would still be able to negotiate within its limits. What was more important was that for the first time in forty years of GATT, negotiation of agriculture was agreed. This was historic.

The new issues

Agriculture was settled before services at Punta. The services negotiations were protracted. Clayton Yeutter handled these himself. Yeutter, the Indian minister and Batista, the Brazilian ambassador from Geneva, stuck at it for hours. Settlement was finally reached. It was along the lines that had been foreshadowed for weeks but it spelt it out in detail: services were to be negotiated but in an entirely separate framework from the GATT negotiations on goods. Two distinct processes had to be created – one for goods and the other for services.

Intellectual property and investment were also very difficult issues. The deal here was that discussion of these issues would take place in a way which did not disrupt the harmony of the process. The developing countries were strongly opposed to negotiations on these issues. They considered that agreement to discuss these issues in the Uruguay Round did not represent a commitment to liberalize. For the Americans it was an achievement that these matters were on the agenda at all. Intellectual property was to become a major issue for the United States.

Punta had been historic. Developing countries had participated actively in negotiating the mandate for the Round. It was as much their round as anybody else's. There was agreement to negotiate on agriculture and services. They were tied. There was a compact that one could not move without the other. It was one of those remarkable meetings where everybody considered that they had achieved something.

Chaper Eleven
INITIAL SPIN OFFS

A new organization

After ministers mandated the four-year trade round in September 1986 at Punta del Este, negotiators returned to Geneva. Before taking their Christmas and annual January skiing break, they had to prepare negotiating plans, settle timetables and select presiding officers for each of the 15 negotiating groups. Once these tasks were out of the way they expected to settle down to the business of preparing and putting forward negotiating proposals. They expected work in GATT to run down as the workload in the trade negotiations built up. To everyone's surprise the workload in GATT increased dramatically. Countries started to bring trade disputes to GATT.

The Uruguay Round had effectively created a new international organization for its four-year life. This would run separately and in parallel with the GATT's own activities. At the apex of the organisation for the negotiations was the Trade Negotiations Committee. All countries participating in the negotiations were members of the committee. Arthur Dunkel chaired it when it was attended by officials. On the special occasions when the committee was attended by ministers the presiding officer would be Enrique Iglesias, the Uruguayan foreign minister who had presided at Punta.

Reporting to the committee, was the Group for Negotiations on Goods (GNG). To it in turn reported the negotiating groups

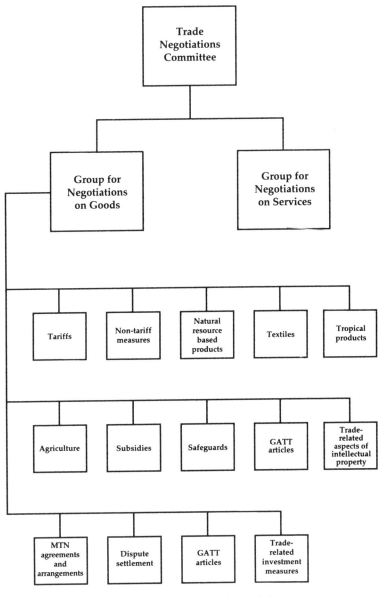

FIGURE 11.1 *Structure of negotiations*

which had been created to handle each of the subject areas inditified by ministers except one. The exception was the Group for Negotiations on Services (GNS). It was not subordinate to the GNG, but of parallel status and reported directly to the Trade Negotiations Committee (see Figure 11.1).

This arrangement reflected the agreement that negotiations over goods and services were to be kept strictly separate so that there could be no possibility of concessions being sought in services in exchange for concessions on offer in the goods negotiations, for example through reductions of tariffs or removal of non-tariff barriers.

GATT had its own structure. Each six weeks or so the council met. This was the main forum of the GATT between the annual meetings of the contracting parties. It received reports from subsidiary bodies set up to deal with *ad hoc* issues. More importantly, it handled trade disputes.

Most delegations in Geneva had not yet been increased to handle the greater workload which the round would inevitably create. It would build up gradually and the normal workload of the GATT was expected to wind down.

A rush to court

One of the declared objectives of the Uruguay Round was to improve GATT's dispute settlement procedures. The system was not in good shape. It had been used infrequently and there had been a handful of damaging non-results. Businessmen in Europe were largely unaware of its existence while those in the United States who were aware of it regarded it as largely ineffective. A negotiating group had been established to improve the rules. Its chairman was one of GATT's most experienced ambassadors, Julio Lacarte-Muro of Uruguay.

Unexpectedly, countries did not wait for the rules to be improved before taking trade disputes to the GATT court. The caseload rose. The United States and the European Community challenged Japanese trade barriers and the barriers of each other; and Japan challenged theirs. In addition agricultural trade barriers were tested and found wanting. The system was coming to life. Clearly the commitment to agree to participate in the multilateral trade negotiation also reflected a renewed interest in using that system to settle trade disputes. The regular meetings of the GATT council became more crowded, more important and more relevant to the world of trade.

The upsurge in disputes brought to GATT bore out the belief among many that the reason why the GATT dispute settlement procedures had fallen into disuse was not necessarily because of fundamental problems with the rules: it was rather that the major trading countries did not find the whole idea to their taste.

In the case of the United States and the European Community, their unwillingness to use the GATT court to settle trade disputes was a reflection of their unwillingness to accept the constraints of operating in a multilateral trade system. As a generality, temporary protection was only allowed under GATT rules in two cases. In the first it had to be demonstrated that an imported product was being dumped below the cost of production and that this was damaging established suppliers. An anti-dumping duty could be imposed to bring the cost of the imported product up to its proper price.

In the second case temporary protection was allowed if there was a surge of competitively, but fairly priced imports. The restrictions had to apply to imports of the same product from all countries and there had to be commitments to phase them out. Other GATT parties had a technical right to compensation for loss of trade as a result of the raising of the barrier. The philosophy was to give the importing country breathing space to re-equip to be able to compete. These were known as the safeguards procedures.

US and EC trade officials knew that over the years they would not be able to satisfy the conditions of these GATT rules to contain competitive imports. Neat and quiet bilateral deals were not possible under these rules. They also made it difficult to threaten action against a particular industry in a particular country and to twist the tail of another government in other areas of the bilateral relationship such as immigration, invest-ment or aid so as to bring the offending trade to heel.

Evolution of attitudes

One of the peculiarities of the GATT disputes system is that the defendant and the plaintiff are also both part judge and jury. Defendant and plaintiff both participate in the key procedural decisions in the process, namely the decision to submit the dispute to adjudication procedures and the decision on whether the measure in question is legal under GATT.

When countries bring a complaint to GATT it is presented to the council which comprises all GATT parties. The council then creates a panel of three, sometimes five, people drawn from delegations which are disinterested and from a list of independent experts maintained by the secretariat.

The complaint is standard – that the GATT rights of the complainant have been nullified. The panel hears the case from each party and any other party which wants to put its point of view, assesses the issues and makes a judgement. The report is then considered by the council. It the panel finds that the measure in question is not permitted under GATT rules, and the council adopts the report, the party which put the measure in place is obliged to remove it.

There is provision for the council to determine compensation if the measure has caused trade damage or if the offending party does not want to remove the measure. These provisions have rarely been used. It is a very strong convention that most countries accept the recommendations of the panels.

Each of the key decisions in the process is taken by consensus by the council. Since the complainant and the defendant is each a member of the council each is in a position to hold up each decision and block the process. The extent to which the system is effective therefore depends entirely on the consent of the parties; and the big players exert a major influence on the shape of that consensus.

In its early years parties to GATT took complaints to it readily. In the 1960s there were almost no cases. The prevailing attitude was to settle disputes pragmatically. The dispute settlement rules were considered unnecessarily confrontational. The situation changed in the early 1970s as the United States started to feel the brunt of sharper competition from Japan. It decided that the GATT dispute procedures should be shored up. They should be used and used legalistically.

A difference of philosophy emerged between the United States and the European Community. The United States argued that the articles of GATT were like laws and the GATT dispute panels should determine whether the measure in question was in accord with the law or not. The Community emphasized arbitration. The process should be used to settle disputes and the dispute panels should be encouraged to help devise solutions.

These positions were not unrelated to substantive trade differences between the United States and the Community. The issue of most frequent contention between them was agricultural trade. Complaints over non-agricultural items were handled efficiently and successfully. But as the level of protection of agricultural trade in the European Community grew and this started to impact on the trade of other countries, the Community did not consider it in its interest that a legalist philosophy of dispute settlement in GATT should be used to rule out some of the underpinnings of the Common Agricultural Policy.

In the late 1970s the GATT court was at its most unpopular with the United States and the European Community. Each used it against the other and neither would accept the result. Perhaps it would have been better if complaints had not been initiated. At least then the authority of the disputes settlement process would not have been diminished. There were several notable cases involving disputes between the United States and the Community. The Community, and then the United States, refused to accept adverse findings by GATT's panel. They used their participation in the process to hold up decisions to accept the reports. Agriculture was at the core of the problem.

This was the nadir of the GATT dispute settlement process. Not only did the GATT rules not fully apply to agriculture; what rules there were were ill defined; and there was an active desire by the Community not to define them further. The European Community and the United States had demonstrated that the process was only satisfactory if it produced results satisfactory to them.

A new utility

Japan has been one of the keys to greater use and acceptance of GATT by the United States and the European Community in the last few years. Smaller countries were always willing to take GATT action against other small countries. However, the credibility of the system depended on recognition of its *de facto* authority by the big players, at first the Community and the United States and then Japan.

The United States and the European Community both successfully took cases against Japan in 1985/6. Some of these cases were very difficult for Japan. In 1986 the United States challenged Japanese restrictions on imports of a range of agricultural products and the European community challenged Japanese restrictions on imports of alcohol, particularly scotch. Japan accepted the outcomes. This was important. The United States and the European Community had shown that they would not necessarily agree to findings that were unacceptable. Japan's attitude set a new moral tone in GATT and effectively challenged the Community and the United States to follow suit.

The Community and the United States began to challenge each other in sensitive areas. The Community and Japan each used the GATT system to pursue their interests in the US dispute with Japan over trade in computer chips (semiconductors). The Americans imposed tariffs on imports from Japan because they claimed that Japan was not sticking to the terms of a bilateral agreement between the United States and Japan over trade in semiconductors. Japan challenged these tariffs in GATT as illegal. There is no doubt they were. Tariffs may not be imposed selectively on imports from individual countries. The United States eased some of the restrictions and Japan did not press its complaint all the way to a panel.

The Community then successfully challenged the legality under GATT of the provisions in the US/Japan semiconductor agreement which required prices to be kept up in third markets. In upholding the EC claim the panel was careful to point out that it had not addressed the consistency of the entire agreement with GATT. It had not been asked to.

Two actions were to strain the preparedness of the big three to accept the GATT disputes system. Their levels of tolerance had been raised by their successes to date and their ability to demonstrate to their industries that trade interests could be delivered through GATT.

Strained to the limits – soya beans

Under enormous pressure from the United States, Japan agreed to open its beef market. When the market is fully opened in the mid–1990s Japan could be importing US$2 billion per annum more than before their restrictions were challenged under GATT. This is probably the largest single act to open a market that any country has taken in one and possibly two decades. Appropriately, delegates in GATT heaped lavish praise on the Japanese. Japan had further upped the moral ante in GATT.

The crunch was coming for the European Community. For some time US soya bean producers had been unhappy about subsidies which the European Community paid its growers. This allowed EC produce to undercut US imports, which had the right to enter the Community duty free. The Community had granted this concesson to the United States in the 1960s when soya bean trade was insignificant. In the late 1980s US exports to the Community were worth about US$2 billion per annum.

The US growers pressed the administration to take a panel against the EC subsidies. Any measure which undermines the value of a bound tariff is illegal. The administration was uneasy. It knew that this case would push EC tolerance to the limit. The Community had said that it was prepared to negotiate on agricultural trade with the United States in the Uruguay Round. It was prepared to argue that its own farmers had to accept cuts provided that it could also be demonstrated that support for US farmers was being cut as well. But the Community had warned about the consequences for its support of GATT and the Uruguay Round if it were challenged through the GATT process while it was negotiating in the Uruguay Round. There is always an amount of bluff in such statements; but how much?

The administration was under domestic pressure. The soya bean producers had triggered the retaliatory procedures under

Section 301 of the US Trade Act. The administration concluded that it was preferable to channel the challenge to the EC measure through GATT so it went ahead and requested a panel to test the validity of the EC measures. The French were outraged. Production of oil-seeds had soared in the Community in recent years. The chief economist at Unilever dubbed it the 'yellowing of Europe', which was the effect to be observed from the window of any aircraft flying over Europe in spring as the yellow rape seed plants burst into flower. Over French opposition, the Community agreed to let the case proceed.

The panel delivered its verdict late in 1989. The measures had to be phased out. Neither the United States nor the Community wanted this issue to blow the negotiations in the Uruguay Round out of the water. In bilateral discussions later in the year, Carla Hills, the US trade representative, and Frans Andriessen, the EC commissioner for external relations, agreed that action to implement the finding would be taken up as part of the multilateral trade negotiations.

Screwdriver assembly

The Community's electronics industry suffered the same pressure of intense competitiveness from Japanese products as industry in the United States. Over the years the Community had employed a variety of means to control the inflow of Japanese products. By 1990 imports of dot matrix printers, photocopiers and CD players from Japan were subject to EC anti-dumping duties. The trade in these three items with the duty added was worth around ECU3 billion.

These duties had been imposed following complaints from EC industry that these and other products from Japan – hydraulic excavators and electronic scales – were being sold below Japanese domestic prices. Japanese manufacturers then started to export the components to subsidiary or joint venture companies in Europe where they were assembled and put on the market for prices close to the price of the imported cousin. EC officials considered that these steps had been taken to get around the earlier duties and imposed penalties which they called an anti-circumvention duty.

Japanese representatives were getting steadily more assertive in GATT. Japan decided to act. It was encouraged by increasing complaints from other Pacific rim economies (Korea, Hong Kong and Singapore) about use by the European Community of anti-dumping to block their imports. Japan lodged a complaint that the EC penalties contravened GATT rules.

The panel found that the Japanese were right. The EC measure was not a duty within the terms of GATT rules. A duty could only be imposed after an investigation and after it had established that dumping had occurred and had caused damage. The EC measure was a tax. It discriminated between products and this was not permitted under GATT. Japan had won its first case in GATT.

It was a blow to the Community. But it was unrepentant. Frans Andriessen, the EC commissioner for external relations, stated that GATT might have said the EC legislation conflicted with GATT rules, but it left the problem of circumvention unresolved. The EC Community's tolerance of the GATT disputes system was stretched to its full limit.

Agriculture in from the cold

Agreement at Punta to negotiate on agriculture was mirrored in GATT through *de facto* extension of the GATT's dispute settlement jurisdiction to agriculture. The US soya-bean case was not the first GATT ruling that the Community had accepted on an agricultural trade issue since the Uruguay round had begun. Early in 1989 Chile had won a ruling that the Community could not impose limits on the quantity of apples that Chile and other exporters of apples from the southern hemisphere could export to it.

Two important ruling against Japanese restrictions on imports of agricultural products had been made. US agricultural restrictions were also challenged. Australia secured a GATT ruling that the basis upon which the United States restricted imports of sugar was not legal under the GATT. The United States, like the Community in the soya-bean case declared that it would make the necessary changes in the process of the Uruguay Round agriculture negotiations.

Even before negotiations in the Uruguay Round to embark on a global liberalization of protection of trade in agriculture had concluded, the Community, the United States and Japan had effectively accepted the extension of GATT's jurisdiction in the area of agricultural trade. More importantly, they had allowed the GATT dispute settlement procedures to be used to achieve a significant degree of trade liberalization. Finally the United States, the Economic Community and Japan elected to use GATT procedures to handle some difficult trade disputes. This was a major sea change. The commitment to liberalization and multilateralism which was implicit in the decision to launch the Uruguay Round negotiations was already being reflected in the restoration of the effectiveness of the GATT itself.

Chapter Twelve
SHOWDOWN AT MONTREAL

'So the Americans and the Community cannot reach agreement on agriculture?', asked Paulo Tarso Fleche de Lima, the head of the Brazilian foreign ministry. 'That is correct.' replied Leopoldo Tettamanti, Argentina's ambassador to GATT, grimly. 'That's it. They cannot do this', said Tarso.

It was 6 o'clock in the afternoon on 8 December 1988. It was the eve of the last day of the conference of ministers that had been convened in Montreal to review mid-term progress in the multilateral trade negotiations. Tettamanti and Tarso, looking drawn like everyone else from two nearly sleepless nights, had arrived at the room at the Montreal conference centre that the Cairns Group had reserved for caucusing.

Michael Duffy, the Australian Trade Minister, had called a meeting of the Group to inform it that, following a last ditch effort which had begun that afternoon, it was clear that the gap between the US and EC negotiating positions on agriculture was unbridgeable. A deal had already been struck on services. What was in prospect was what the ministers of the Latin American countries had agreed a month before in Geneva must not happen: that progress would be made in the new areas but that none would be made in the old neglected and protected areas of trade.

The ministers and officials in the Cairns Group quickly conferred and decided that individual members of the group would do what they believed they had to do. Everybody knew what this meant. The Latin American members of the Group – Argentina, Brazil, Colombia, Chile and Uruguay – were about to become the shock troops of the Uruguay Round. They went into the 'Green Room' steering group of ministers which was being chaired by Uruguay's foreign minister, Ricardo Zerbino, and announced that they would not support any agreements reached in any other area until agreements were reached on agriculture. Time had run out in Montreal. The Uruguay Round had been blocked.

Securing a mid-term review

The idea of a mid-term review was Clayton Yeutter's. He reasoned that it was not credible to Congress or the international business community for governments to negotiate for four years to liberalize trade before any results emerged. Others agreed and saw the sense of erecting milestones for the negotiators. They had to be given targets to meet within the four-year programme.

Yeutter understood that for people to come around to new ideas they had to be given time to chew them over. Some key players were still only adjusting to the idea that negotiations were to start and were far from committed to them; and now he was trying to force them to start to think about the outcome. It was clear from developments so far that major decisions had to be taken by consensus. Achieving consensus among over one hundred countries was laborious. The process is like the wave effect caused by dropping a pebble into a pond. The idea is dropped at a central point or with some central players. More and more are brought into the expanding circle until it encompasses all participants.

Early in 1987 Yeutter advanced the idea of a conference of ministers to meet halfway through the Round to secure early results, an 'early harvest', from the negotiations. Yeutter raised the idea initially with Arthur Dunkel and at one of the regular quadrilateral informal discussions between the Community, Canada, Japan and the United States. He also floated it at the meeting of trade ministers which was held at Lake Taupo, New Zealand in March 1987. This was one of the regular series of informal meetings of trade ministers which were inaugurated by Bill Brock in 1983 in part to generate support for a round of trade negotiations.

At the Taupo meeting which Mike Moore chaired Yeutter explained the concept of the mid-term review. There would have to a package of results which respected the need to balance the old and the new areas. Yeutter was open to suggestions but thought himself that there could be agreements on:

1. Improvements to the dispute settlement procedures.
2. Arrangements to strengthen the GATT system.
3. The framework of a services agreement.
4. How tariff reductions might be achieved.
5. Interim agreements to reduce protection in agriculture.

The European Community expressed caution. Willy de Clercq, the European Commissioner for External Affairs, a Belgian who sported a bow tie and a splendid shock of white hair, spelt out the Community's reservations in orthodox fashion. It might be a mistake to try to secure early results. The effort might fail and damage the credibility of the Round. Agriculture could not be put on a 'fast-track'. Efforts to liberalize in one sector could not move faster than efforts to liberalize in others. There had to be 'globality'.

'Globality' had become the byword of the EC approach to the negotiations. It meant that the negotiation had to be regarded as a single enterprise. No particular area of the negotiations could be singled out for special treatment. The most extreme interpretation of globality was usually heard from French diplomats. They would contend that all areas of the negotiations had to proceed at exactly the same pace. This was not practical. Some areas of the negotiation were relatively unimportant and little would or could be achieved in them. The Americans interpreted globality as 'Eurospeak' for saying that little was to be allowed to happen in the negotiations on agriculture.

Some developing countries also had reservations about Yeutter's idea, especially those which were dug in over the issue of inclusion of new issues in the negotiations. They supported globality but for a reason which was the obverse of the French position – under no circumstances was the issue of services to get out ahead of the other issues. Predictably, the idea of securing interim results was supported by ministers from the countries which had most actively worked to get the Round started.

Yeutter had sown the seed of his idea. As the concept took hold it was progressively accepted. It was canvassed through the various consultative groups in Geneva. Dunkel carried it through his informal consultative mechanisms, canvassed it with heads of delegations and then in early 1988, the Trade Negotiations Committee accepted his proposal that ministers meet at Montreal at the end of that year.

The date and venue had been agreed, but not what the outcome of the meeting ought to be. The time between the beginning of 1987 and the mid-term review in December 1988 was spent getting negotiating proposals out on the table, agreeing on what the mid-term package should contain and, finally, preparing for and then negotiating the content of the mid-term package in the months leading up to and at Montreal.

New networks

The emergence of new interests and collaboration between various groups of countries meant that the dynamics of this negotiation were different from previous trade rounds. The driving forces in the Tokyo Round of trade negotiations had been the United States and the other three quadrilaterals. The objectives for the Tokyo Round were prepared following discussions among the United States, Japan and the European Community. They announced that the negotiations were to begin and everyone else was invited to participate.

When those negotiations were finally brought to a belated conclusion in 1979 it was as a result of intense negotiations among the United States, Canada, the European Community and Japan. They presented the results of their negotiations first to the rest of the industrialized countries and then to the developing countries virtually on a take it or leave it basis. This was accepted, but only begrudgingly by the countries participating in the trade round. The rich were behaving as if GATT were their club.

The driving force for the Uruguay Round was initially the United States, the EFTA countries and exporters from the Asian/Pacific region and Latin America. Japan has always supported the Round strongly but on substantive issues tended to be reactive. The Community's enthusiasm for the Round was slow to be kindled. Collaboration between developing and industrialized countries was one of the notable features of the Uruguay Round.

While industrialized countries and developing countries continued to use established forums for consultation among themselves, other important networks had emerged. The Cairns Group had been the most visible manifestation of the preparedness of countries to collaborate on the basis of trade interests and across established group lines. Other groups were emerging. For the previous year, Asian/Pacific countries had met regularly to monitor developments in Geneva and periodically in capitals after meeting initially in Hobart, Australia in 1985. This group did not collaborate on common proposals. But it met to review developments from the Asian/Pacific perspective.

Another important group was formed after delegations returned to Geneva from Montreal. The Swiss ambassador, Pierre Louis Girard, invited to lunch at the de la Paix hotel, which overlooks the old Geneva port, the core of countries which had decamped to the EFTA building in July and laid the basis of the outcome at Punta. The group was balanced between developing and industrialized countries. It included Australia, Canada, Colombia, Hong Kong, Hungary, Pakistan, New Zealand, Singapore, South Korea, Sweden, Uruguay, and Zaire. It did not include the European Community, the United States or Japan. They felt pretty good. They felt, justifiably, that had they not acted as they did in July the Round might have been stillborn.

The group took the hotel's name. It began to meet regularly with a common commitment to maintain the momentum of the Round. Initially it focused on the process. But as work in groups progressed, members of the group prepared and submitted collective proposals for the negotiations. This consolidated the practice begun by the Cairns Group of collaboration across the old established divisions between developed and developing countries. They submitted proposals on tariffs, non-tariff measures, the functioning of GATT, dispute settlement and intellectual property.

An important group also emerged towards the end of the year for discussions on services. It became known as the Rolle group after the small Genèvois town near Geneva where the first discussions were held. A quartet of delegates were the prime movers – Meg McDonald, an Australian, Jo Tyndall, a New Zealander, Carl Leifland, a Swede and Elaine Feldman, a Canadian. The group comprised those developing countries which were wary about, but not in principle opposed to, negotiations on services, such as Argentina, Thailand and Korea, the big three, and other industrialized countries. This group played a very important role in extending understanding of the services issues among delegations and its internal working papers were influential in the work of the services group.

Getting going

Arthur Dunkel's first job in 1987 was to get the negotiating groups going. He organized the appointment of presiding officers for the groups and saw quickly to finalization of their negotiating plans. He achieved agreement on these matters in the green room. This is a small conference room on the first floor of the GATT building in Geneva near the Director-General's office. The walls are wallpapered halfway up in a khaki green. The conference table seats 18 comfortably.

It was used for an essential part of the negotiations which came to be dubbed the 'green room process'. Formal decisions concerning the trade round were taken in the Trade Negotiations Committee. It had 105 members and could not be used effectively except to adopt decisions over which consensus had already been reached. Dunkel used the green room for consultations with a core of key delegations and his two deputies, Madan Mathur and Charles Carlisle.

Negotiating proposals in each of the negotiating areas slowly started to come on to the table. Agriculture gave the process momentum in 1987. At the Venice summit of the major industrialized powers in the middle of the year, the heads of government of the big 7 agreed that their governments should all put major proposals on the table by the end of the year. Proposals could have been expected from the United States and Canada, but this decision ensured that they came as well from the European Community and Japan. These submissions demonstrated that these governments meant business in the Round. It encouraged efforts by others.

Discussions on services were desultory and depressing. It was clear that those countries which had most strongly opposed negotiations on services had not changed their minds. Throughout 1987 most of the discussions were a dialogue of the deaf. In the meantime, the US Coalition of Services Industries embarked on a systematic programme to stimulate private sector interest in the liberalization of services in a number of countries. The US intellectual property interests began to intensify their efforts. They concentrated first on asserting their influence with the US government. They also worked to stimulate interest in sister industries in other countries, particularly in the industrialized world.

The package

Thinking started to crystallize on what would constitute a reasonable package of results for consideration at Montreal. Dispute settlement and the functioning of the GATT system (awkwardly, but according to the local wits appropriately, known as FOGS) were seen as less controversial areas where it would be sensible to reach early agreements to clear the decks a little before the end of the Round.

The United States and the Cairns Group were insistent that there had to be a significant result in agriculture. The United States and the European Community were equally insistent that there had to be significant progress in services. Developing countries focused on tropical products as an area where the industrialized countries should liberalize to the benefit of developing countries. There was also general agreement that the basis for the negotiations to reduce tariffs should be settled so that after Montreal the work on the detail of the tariff reductions could begin.

To maintain faith with the principle of 'globality' for those to whom it was important, it was accepted that there would be a report to the ministers in every area of the negotiation. In those areas other than the ones already mentioned these reports were not intended to do any more than carry out the obligation to report.

Preparing for Montreal

In mid-1988, Dunkel asked the presiding officers of the negotiating groups to prepare, by early November, reports to be considered by the ministers at Montreal in December. Some groups would not be able to settle differences. So he also planned a marathon negotiating session for mid-November in the green room to go over the reports again.

Some chairmen had an impossible task. Lars Arnell, the Swedish ambassador, was chairman of the intellectual property group. The developing countries might have agreed at Punta to include this subject in the Round. But they had no intention of negotiating; at least not yet. The opening positions of the United States and the Swiss were to insist that negotiations begin. Arnell made Herculean efforts to coax and cajole representatives to common ground and made himself unpopular in the process. Felipe Jaramillo who chaired the services group had similar problems. At least delegates were talking but there was also a great deal of stalling. The hardline developing countries led by India and Brazil were not even conceding the point that there should be an international agreement.

Storm clouds were gathering over the agriculture discussions. Both Art de Zeeuw, chairman of the agriculture group, and the Cairns Group had been urging the United States and the European Community to begin to negotiate. De Zeeuw had produced a masterly working paper drawing on the positions of the major players. The issues were complex and politically sensitive. No agreement of any significance could be reached at Montreal unless there was a protracted period of negotiation. The United States and the Community would not engage. At a meeting of the Cairns Group in Geneva late in 1988, Leopoldo Tettamanti reported on a trip he had just taken to Buenos Aires. 'With the President we reviewed the Uruguay Round. If the US and EC do not make progress on agriculture at the mid-term review in Montreal, Argentina will not support results in other area of the Round.'

Jules Katz, who was later to be appointed by Carla Hills as one of her deputies, had pushed the Gatt functioning group hard. He had virtually secured agreement to biennial GATT meetings of ministers. More importantly, he had near agreement on adoption in the GATT of a process of regular surveillance of trade policies of GATT parties. Many developing countries were uncomfortable with the surveillance scheme. They did not have traditions of open government. There had also been efforts to slow down the work because the Americans had been pushing in services and intellectual property. Katz had been impatient with some of the deliberate stalling and there were some bruised egos.

Julio Lacarte was also facing some tactical stalling in the dispute settlement group. He had also to contend with some rather bizarre argumentation that a different standard of justice should apply to developing countries. Another problem was that Japan and the European Community wanted to make an issue at Montreal of use by the United States of Section 301. They were not ready to concede positions to get agreement and neither therefore was anyone else.

Agreement on how to negotiate even tariff reductions was proving elusive. The United States would not agree to a common formula for reductions. They wanted to be able to negotiate reductions in individual tariffs but were prepared to agree that cuts should average 30 per cent. The European Community, Japan and Canada all insisted that tariffs should be cut by a common formula, as they were in the Tokyo Round. The de la Paix group countries made a valiant effort to straddle these differences. The only bright spot was tropical products. The industrialized countries accepted that they should reduce their barriers as an incentive to developing countries. All indicated that they would make reductions, although they were small.

The green room in Geneva

Arthur Dunkel had set a week aside to resolve all these issues. He would apply the techniques of negotiation by attrition. It was about the only time life was ever uncomfortable for diplomats in Geneva. Over several long days and nights, he presided over an endless session of negotiation, going through the report from each negotiating group, one after the other. He had his staff bring in hamburgers and pizza. He occasionally took a break handing the chair to Mathur or Carlisle. The ambassadors and representatives had their specialist staff on hand to advise or take the seat in the green room as the subject matter changed. The foyer was crowded with tired, but generally good humoured diplomats.

Of the 14 subject areas of the negotiations there was an unwritten consensus that the areas in which efforts would be made to achieve new, substantive agreements were agriculture, services, dispute settlement, the functioning of GATT, tariffs and tropical products. The reports for Montreal were knocked into shape. Only a few critical points of difference were left in the proposals on dispute settlement and functioning of the GATT. However the tariff paper looked as if it had been put together by a systems engineer.

A serious process of negotiation had at last begun over services, although the paper which emerged had so many brackets and unresolved alternatives that it was nearly incomprehensible. Intellectual property remained a major problem. No agreement was possible and the report to ministers contained four different proposals. The time spent on textiles began to grow. By virtual tacit consent the issue had been left largely undiscussed during the first two years of the Round. It would become more important after Montreal. The United States had indicated that it was able to consider the idea of liberalizing textiles, but not very specifically. It was recognized that there was no point attempting to address textiles until a pattern of other issues falling into place was emerging at Montreal. There was a general consensus that safeguards was a nut to be cracked after Montreal, not before. India insisted, however, in maintaining one point of disagreement to ensure the issue was remitted to ministers.

The position on agriculture had not improved. Discussions on this subject had been carried on in an informal group of 10 countries called the Morges Group. It had been created from among the leading agricultural traders a few years before as forum for open and unreported discussions on agriculture. It took its name from a small town north of Geneva on Lake Léman where its first meetings had taken place. Its members were usually represented by senior officials from capitals.

At the final discussion in this forum before Montreal, Dan Amstutz, the US negotiator on agriculture and Guy Legras, head of DG VI, the agricultural directorate in the European Commission in Brussels, faced each other across the table. The US position was that all agricultural barriers should be eliminated within ten years. The Community had proposed that short-term action be taken to stabilize global markets. They simply repeated these positions to each other. There was no negotiation. The negotiators had left their ministers in Montreal a tall order.

Montreal

With Canada as host the mid-term review began on 5 December at Montreal's state of the art but cavernous conference centre. Enrique Iglesias had retired as foreign minister of Uruguay and his successor Ricardo Zerbino presided over the meeting. He tasked individual ministers to take responsibility for trying to resolve outstanding differences in the difficult areas. They were then to bring the issue to a green room style forum comprising ministers and their senior advisers.

Anita Gradin, Sweden's trade minister, was responsible for services. Armed with a text on which Arnell had done a lot of work she began consulting ministers about their views. Over two days she reduced the number of disagreements until she was ready to put the final unresolved issues into the green room. Discussions on services had advanced dramatically in six weeks. There was now consensus that there should be a services agreement. There was nearly agreement on what major issues should be covered in an agreement. A work plan for the rest of the negotiations was laid out. In the green room, agreement was reached fairly quickly. There were whoops of delight from the

US delegation when it was finished. Clayton Yeutter could start to see progress on an issue which he had pushed almost single handedly at Punta two years earlier.

There were long faces in the agriculture camp. The services negotiations had succeeded because there had been a willingness to negotiate. This was missing in the agriculture negotiations. Zerbino himself presided over initial discussions on agriculture. Then on 7 December he asked Michael Duffy to manage a small group to handle agriculture. The United States and the European Community disagreed fundamentally over the long-term objective of agricultural reform. The US position was complete liberalization, the Community said gradual reductions of support.

It was clear that until this were resolved, there was no point in trying to tackle other issues. Early in the evening of Wednesday 7 December Duffy suggested that the two exchange positions and develop a common position on the long-term objective. Then he would have the group look at this and work through the other issues. Of those the most important was some form of immediate freeze on existing levels of protection. The agriculture negotiators marked time around the conference rooms waiting for the United States and the European Community. Around 11.30 p.m. that evening, Peter Field, Duffy's senior Australian official ran into Jean Marc Lucq, a Frenchman who was head of the GATT agriculture division. They were old skiing chums. Field asked how the Community and the United States were going. They weren't, replied Lucq.

The Community and the United States had exchanged written positions on the understanding they would meet after reading them. Lyng had looked at the EC proposal. He did not see any shift in the EC position and could not see the sense of talking to the Community. He went to bed. The Community's negotiators were huddled in the coffee shop. Duffy sent out messages that he wanted the agriculture negotiators assembled. They met around 1.00 a.m. The following two hours have their place of honour in the dismal history in the previous of three and a half decades of protection of trade in agriculture.

Dick Lyng and Frans Andriessen, the leaders of the two richest administrations in the world, which between them directly controlled budgets that spent a minimum annually of US$50 billion supporting their farmers, bickered like schoolboys over who was more serious about reform. They could not agree the long-term objective of the negotiations. They were not positioned to negotiate. After two hours Duffy adjourned the discussions. There was no point in prolonging the agony.

At around 7.00 a.m. on Thursday Zerbino called a green room meeting. The conference was to end the next day. Agreements had been reached on reforms to the dispute settlement procedures of the GATT and on introduction of a mechanism for surveillance of trade policies. It had been agreed that tariff reductions should average 30 per cent and there was now a clear framework for negotiating a services agreement. Discussions were still proceeding on intellectual property and appeared to be making headway. Textiles and safeguards had not yet been considered.

The issue was agriculture. De Clercq proposed that ministers simply agree to direct negotiators in Geneva to continue working on agriculture. Good results had already been achieved in other areas and the Round still had two years to run. The response was sharp. Moore set the tone. This was unacceptable. Gradin, Sabin from Thailand and Grinspun from Argentina argued that the issue was so important that there had to be another attempt at agreement. Zerbino extended the conference one more day until 9 December.

Duffy reconvened the Group at 2.00 p.m. It was already nearly too late. Time was needed for the administrative formalities. Other issues beside the long-term objective for agriculture had yet to be addressed. These were difficult and sensitive and the way had not been prepared in Geneva.

There was now a negotiation. A genuine effort was made to find a common position on the long term. The Community and the United States tried new formulae. For two hours a number of approaches were tried. Cairns Group countries offered a variety of approaches to bridge the gap between the United States and the Community. It was unbridgeable. The negotiators had not come prepared to be sufficiently accommodating. There was no point in proceeding. Mike Moore challenged Lyng and Andriessen. 'What are you going to do now?' They hadn't the slightest idea. Duffy closed the meeting.

The Cairns Group met. As chairman of the Group Duffy knew that not all the members of the Group would have been prepared to veto the results in the other areas. Confrontation was not a feature of the politics of some members. The Latin Americans had the strongest position. They would deny consensus on the other issues. The rest of the group would not undermine this position.

Zerbino reconvened the green room discussions. No politician likes to declare failure. The mood in the EC and US camps was to base the outcome of the meeting on the substantial agreements negotiated in the other areas and to remit agriculture to the continuing negotiating process. This was acceptable to a number of other delegations. The five Latin members of the Cairns Group said that there could be no agreement on any issue under these circumstances. This would have doomed the agriculture negotiations to secondary status and to failure.

The politics of GATT had changed. It was no longer a system which operated on what was agreed among the quadrilaterals. Dunkel then proposed that the ministers give the process a stay of execution. The outcome would be held over until the first week in April. Negotiators in Geneva would focus on the outstanding issues, particularly agriculture.

There were other outstanding issues – intellectual property, textiles and safeguards. Progress had been made on the first two issues but when it was clear that agriculture was not going to be settled work stopped. No final effort had been made to settle the safeguards question. It was agreed that these issues should also be addressed in Geneva. At the formal closing of the Montreal conference of 9 December, the Trade Negotiations Committee adjourned for four months.

Back to Geneva

What now began was what should have happened in the lead up to Montreal. The United States and the European Community began seriously to address the agriculture issues. They both moved from their more rigid positions, particularly the United States. They agreed that the long-term objective of the agriculture negotiations would be to reduce support for agriculture substantially in order to reduce and prevent distortions to trade. This was significant. The Community had never agreed to this before.

There was also agreement not to increase existing levels of protection. Since agricultural prices were buoyant this was relatively easy for both parties. The commitment had plenty of loopholes but it was a statement of bona fides to negotiate seriously in the rest of the Round. The package was settled at a quiet meeting at the EC delegation between Warren Lavorel, one of the best US trade negotiators (Amstutz had not been reappointed by the Bush Administration), Legras and Field, who represented the Cairns Group.

The negotiations on intellectual property were difficult. Developing countries were still very unhappy about having to deal with this subject. They were prepared to consider negotiations for new commitments but would not yet concede that they should be linked to the GATT system. This was an advance. The mandate for the textiles negotiations was made tighter. The aim of bringing textiles back into GATT system and liberalizing the regime was more clearly stated. The developing countries were also starting to behave more forcefully. The mandate for safeguards was settled quickly. This was never a controversial question.

By April Dunkel had his package. The Montreal process ended up a resounding success. Interim results had been achieved. And significant progress had been made in the two most controversial issues – agriculture and services. There is no doubt that had the Latin American Cairns Group countries had not taken the stand they did, Montreal would have sounded the death knell of the Uruguay Round. The architect of the strategy, Leopoldo Tettamanti, was a new hero of the Uruguay Round.

Chapter Thirteen
FIXING GATT –
old markets

One of the major strategic objectives of the Uruguay Round was to strengthen the GATT trading system by re-opening markets which had been excluded from the multilateral trading system. Significant sectors of trade had been removed from the system of GATT trade rules over the past three decades. This had been done legally, by writing different rules for different sectors, as in the case of textiles and to a certain extent agriculture, or by fiat, such as in steel, electronics, automobiles and agriculture as well, where the GATT rules and principles have been ignored.

A relatively new phenomenon has also emerged in recent years. It is the administration of procedures allowed under GATT in such a way that they protect domestic industry and the end result is protective in a way never intended by GATT. This could be called procedural protectionism. It is most manifest in administration of anti-dumping measures.

Every issue of concern in international trade is on the table in the Uruguay Round. The process of revival of relevance of GATT and the strengthening of international commitments to open markets does not require that all the issues on the agenda are addressed or that those that are addressed are done so with finality. What needs to be demonstrated is a clear beginning of a retreat from protectionism. In the most heavily protected sectors, agriculture and textiles, tens of billions of dollars are being lost both in economies which are being protected as well as in the economies which are being denied the opportunities to export.

171

Agriculture – now a subject for liberalization

Apart from the disproportionate amount of political power exerted by farmers, the other thing that is common about protection of agriculture in the industrialized world is the phenomenal amount of money that is lost. The OECD has calculated that if there were full liberalization of agriculture in the OECD the gain to its economies would be US$45 billion per annum. If developing countries liberalized at the same time, the gain to them would be US$18 billion per annum. The opening of markets in the West would provide great benefits to agricultural exporters outside Europe and the United States. Even a gradual opening of markets would have a dramatic effect on the patterns of global trade.

Greatest pressures against the opening of the market come from the dairy industry. This is the most heavily protected sector in every country of the world except New Zealand. Compared to total production the amount of dairy produce that is traded across borders is relatively small. There are very wide differences in costs of production between the most efficient producers (New Zealand) and the least efficient producers (the European Community and Canada). The EC beef market is heavily restricted against the much more efficient producers in Latin America. Opening agricultural markets could provide dramatic increases in export earnings for heavily indebted countries like Argentina and Brazil.

Rationality does not have a great role when it comes to the cost of protection. If it did there would be far less. While governments have announced that they will negotiate for change in the Uruguay Round, achieving the change will be difficult. The major threat to success in the negotiations over agriculture lies within the political processes of the European Community and the United States. There are internal pressures within both not to commit themselves to cuts. There are budgetary pressures to make cuts but these do not carry the same political clout.

The forces against reduction of protection in the Community, the United States and Japan are probably better organized than domestic forces arguing for change. Farm groups in the United

States and Europe would have cheered if agriculture had been allowed to fall off the table at Montreal. Counterbalancing this as a factor supporting change is the dynamics of the relationship between the Community and the United States. The trade of each in international markets is sufficiently intertwined for it to be feasible for one to start to cut farm support significantly only if the other is doing so at the same time. This is the classical situation in which substantial multilateral trade liberalization has taken place in the past. Administrations were able to argue to domestic constituencies that cuts had to be made because others in similar positions in other parts of the world were making similar cuts. Given the importance of Japan as an export market for US agricultural products, Japan needs to be added to this political equation as well.

Classical differences in approach exist between the United States and the European Community. While there is a long tradition of government support for US farmers going back to Wilson and Roosevelt, market forces are understood in significant sectors of US agriculture. This reflects a strong, general US disposition to let the market dictate production and trade and to keep the government out. This is the basic position of the American Farm Bureau Federation, one of the largest farm organizations in the United States. The original proposal which the United States put on the table late in 1987 was that all forms of support for agriculture should be eliminated by the year 2000. It was supported by the US farm sector, although some heavily protected US agriculture interests, like the sugar lobby, went along with this knowing that the European Community could never buy such a radical approach.

The Community does not have a strong common commitment to the market and in the case of agriculture there is no significant EC farm organization which supports a free market. Outside the United Kingdom and the Netherlands there is almost no tradition of market forces influencing agricultural production and trade in the Community. In the United Kingdom this tradition seems to be weakening as a result of the succour of the CAP. The Community's approach to change is to do it gradually, so gradually that sometimes it does not succeed.

The proposal which the Community tabled at the end of 1987 was so modest as almost to match obversely the radicalism of the US proposal. It proposed that short term action be taken to stabilize markets in the key commodities which accounted for most agricultural trade, and that after that other matters should be considered. Probably this was all the Community was capable of at that time since it was in the middle of reforming the operation of the CAP. The Community placed budgetary limits on the CAP programmes. But to agree to put a ceiling on budgets was not the same as agreeing to start allowing market forces to determine production. This was still not within the realm of EC policy.

The initial proposal for the negotiations which the Cairns Group put out in late 1987 provided a bridge between the Community and United States. It endorsed the radical US approach for long-term reform. It recommended short-term action to freeze support as an initial step in the long-term process. The Cairns framework was what was ultimately used for the mid-term outcome from Montreal. The Cairns Group approach to reform was that it had to include reform of GATT rules to prevent a resurgence of protection of agricultural trade, opening of markets, elimination of subsidies and the cutback of general support for agriculture.

These divergent approaches all had to be accommodated. There was agreement at Montreal that there should be progressive reductions in agricultural support. The issue for the negotiators of GATT was how to achieve them. After Montreal the United States refined its approach. It no longer argued that barriers should be eliminated over a ten-year period, but proposed that all barriers to agricultural trade should be converted to tariffs over time and that the tariffs should then be reduced to very low levels. The European Community advanced its position and proposed that an index be developed which would measure the level of support of agriculture – fixed against standard measures of world prices so that there was a common standard of comparison—and that all countries should then agree to reduce these indexes by common percentages. The Cairns Group proposed that a combination of both approaches be used to reduce protection.

The formulae that have been developed are all excessively technical. Final agreements will need to be simpler or they will not be easily saleable to the farm constituencies, particularly the

US Congress. The politics are difficult. The easiest outcome for the Community would be one which enabled it to maintain the programme of reform put in place by Andriessen in 1988. There are pressures from EC farmers to lift these restrictions. Such an outcome would also allow the Community to hold the share of international markets which it won through the extensive subsidization between the mid–1970s and the mid–1980s. The European Community also wants to 're-balance' certain levels of protection. By this it means raising tariffs in some areas, such as feed stocks and oilseeds. An outcome like this would not liberalize international trade in agriculture.

There are key political desiderata. Agreements on agriculture will need to result in identifiable reductions in support. This will have to be achieved in such a way that administrations in Brussels, Washington and Tokyo will each be able to point out to its farm groups that protection of farming is reducing in other countries, particularly in the other big two. They will need to bring about reductions in the use of export subsidies. No other result will be acceptable to the United States and the Cairns Group. And the agreements will need to lead to a greater influence for market forces as the determinants of production and trade in agriculture.

It took nearly thirty years for international markets for trade in manufactured goods to reach the relatively open state they now enjoy, notwithstanding the number of exceptions that have been created. The current level of excessive protection of agriculture is probably akin to that which existed in markets for manufactures forty years ago. It is reasonable to assume that the process of cuts in agricultural protection will need to be similarly steady over a period of at least two decades. A review of the results of the Uruguay Round will be necessary within five years in order to accelerate the pace of reduction. This was the pattern with the early trade rounds of the GATT.

The consequence of Montreal is that a decision about whether or not to commit to cuts cannot be left to the farm officials and farm lobbies alone. Dilatoriness on their part now threatens the entire prospects for global liberalization that sit within the Uruguay Round.

The heyday of agricultural protectionism in the European Community is past. The Common Agricultural Policy is no longer the primary and most tangible expression of European integration. Among the panoply of seminal issues facing the European Community, the reconstruction of Eastern Europe has pushed the relative importance of supporting the small European farmer well down the totem pole. More significantly, the Community will need money to support the democratization and economic liberalization of Eastern Europe. The greater this need becomes the less satisfactory will be the fact that more than half the EC budget – in 1988 – was spent on the Common Agricultural Policy. In addition, pressures are building in Europe against intensive farming on environmental grounds.

As the Community gradually reduces the proportion of funds spent on the CAP, it will be critical that agreements have been entered into in GATT which carry commitment to giving a greater role to market forces to shape this changing environment. The challenge facing the United States is to pull its agriculture off the teat of government dependence to which it has become accustomed and restore its traditional strength – international competitiveness.

Textiles – the second challenge

William Cline, from the Washington based Institute for International Economics, has calculated that consumers in the United States pay out annually US$135,000 to maintain each job in the textiles industry and US$82,000 for each in the apparel industry. The average wage in these jobs is US$12,000 per annum. If apparel workers were put on permanent vacation at full pay it would cost consumers only one-seventh of what they pay now.

It is clear that exports from developing countries are constrained by the MFA. Recent estimates are that developing country exports of textiles to OECD countries could rise by around 80 per cent and exports of clothing by between 90 and 130 per cent if the trade were fully liberalized. Calculation of the effect of liberalization on individual developing country exporters is difficult because of the way in which quotas distort trade. It is conventionally argued that the major textile and clothing exporters, Korea, Hong Kong and Taiwan, would have a smaller share of global trade if India, China and Pakistan had un-restrained access to the markets of the industrialized world, particularly for clothing.

The clothing and textile industries in the three boom economies have shown remarkable responsiveness to the artificial shifts in markets that have been created through the regular changes to the quotas administered under the MFA. It is likely that liberalization would accelerate the trend that is already in place for clothing manufacturers in the East Asian growth economies to move further up the value-added chain and to compete more with the higher cost, higher quality manufacturers in Japan, Europe and the United States.

There is a category of small developing country manufacturers which may suffer if liberalization is too rapid. These are the small countries in Asia, Latin America and the Caribbean where industries have been developed solely to service the markets created by the trade restrictions under the MFA. Often these businesses are capitalized by companies based in Korea or Hong Kong which have exhausted their country's entitlement to export to the United States or the European Community and have invested in a small country whose exports are only lightly restrained.

At Montreal, the ministers agreed that the 'modalities' for integrating the MFA were to be negotiated. A lawyer examining the text of the agreement would be cautious about exactly what the commitment amounted to. Unlike the case with agriculture, there is no actual commitment to reduce the level of protection.

Shifting the MFA arrangements into the GATT open market system will be difficult. Under the MFA, industrialized countries negotiate bilateral agreements to restrict the quantity of imports from each developing country. These arrangements usually set quotas for the amount of trade that is permitted in the textile or clothing item concerned. Making these arrangements consistent with GATT would require replacing these various trade barriers with tariffs. This would significantly change the pattern of trade in most items. A quota gives a guaranteed amount of trade to the importer, which is entitled to trade inside it. A tariff lets any exporter into a market provided it can compete with the domestic product.

There are those who believe that there are so many vested interests in keeping the MFA arrangements unchanged that governments will not be able to resist the pressures not to change. The United States has proposed that each industrialized country in the MFA replace the existing system of item quotas for each developing country with one large global quota for each item. Every country which wanted to export would have to compete on price inside that quota. The quota would be extended by a fixed percentage each year until it encompassed all trade and was no longer necessary.

No one else supports this approach. The European Community is strongly opposed. EC clothing and textile exports to the United States would be restricted for the first time. They would have to compete with imports from developing countries. Developing countries do not like it either. It was rejected by the 22-member bureau of developing country textile and clothing exporters. They would suddenly find themselves in open competition for part of a share of the global quota. Within the developing countries there are wide differences in levels of efficiency. Cheaper and more efficient exporters like China would increase their share very rapidly.

The developing countries propose that each individual quota under the MFA should be expanded by a certain percentage every year. This would initially still give them guaranteed access and time to adjust gradually to greater competition. Eventually the quota would not be needed since all trade would be covered. The EC approach is similar.

No formula for overnight liberalization is feasible. But some agreement that begins the process of the gradual replacement of the quota system by tariffs will be necessary for the success of the Round. Nevertheless the outcome will be measured by two criteria. Does the agreement mean that a process of gradual conversion of MFA measures into GATT tariffs has begun? And will the agreement lead to a liberalization of trade? The outcome will have to be assessed as meeting these criteria if it is to be judged successful.

Safeguarding or protecting

In the mid–1970s, the United States and then the European Community began to institute controls on imports of steel, television sets, video cassette recorders, machine tools and automobiles from Japan and to a lesser extent from Korea and Taiwan. They are used instead of the GATT mechanisms which exist to enable countries either to contend with damaging, under-cost pricing (anti-dumping arrangements) or to impose temporary barriers to allow time to restore competitiveness to industry (safeguards arrangements).

These arrangements are known in trade jargon as 'grey area' measures because there is no provision for them in GATT and the users of them point out that they have not been ruled illegal under GATT. The legal distinction is nice but there is no doubt that the measures contravene the market principles of GATT. All the measures distort the market and inhibit the operation of the pricing mechanism to a degree that use of the GATT mechanisms would not.

These grey area measures are among the more notorious of non-tariff barriers to trade. Technical doublespeak is used to describe them. Between 1982 and 1985 Japan made 'forecasts' (that is, announced self-imposed quotas) of the numbers of video cassette players that would be exported into the Community and lifted the price to that of the competing European model. The European consumer continued to show a distinct preference for the Japanese VHS and Beta systems over the Philips/Grundig video 2000 system and ended up paying 15 per cent more than they would have otherwise.

In the UK the British Radio Industry and the Electronics Industries Association agreed to a voluntary restraint arrangement under which Japanese exports were held to 10 per cent of the UK market. This has been operating since 1973. Companies also agreed to orderly marketing arrangements. These schemes usually emerge from a suggestion by officials of the importing country and are then proposed by the exporting industry. The Japanese Ministry of Trade and Industry (MITI) frequently monitors (checks that informally agreed levels are not exceeded) the level of exports of the industry concerned.

The peculiar terminology indicates, protestations from government officials notwithstanding, that at least the collaborators in these arrangements appreciate that they are not reputable from the standpoint of open market trade. The general effect of these arrangements is protection, which was the intention behind them. As ever, the consumer pays more since the market cannot properly set the price, and the protected industries are left uncompetitive.

Why were GATT mechanisms not used? The simple answer is that they are not convenient. Few things that are painful are. The anti-dumping procedures are usually not quick and injury has to be proved. The safeguards procedures are also public; the adverse effects of the imports has to be demonstrated; and trading partners have a right to be compensated for loss of trade arising from temporary barriers.

Review of the safeguards procedures is on the agenda of the Uruguay Round. They were on the table in the Tokyo Round but discussions went nowhere. A major issue then, as now, was the desire of the European Community to alter GATT procedures to permit temporary barriers to be applied selectively on the source of the import – for example to restrict imports of automobiles from Japan but not the United States. The primary EC preoccupation was Japan.

Selective imposition of trade barriers was strongly opposed by a number of smaller trading countries. They argued that to allow this would fatally undermine the most fundamental of GATT's open market principles that trade barriers must not discriminate between sources of imports. The GATT principle is that the only barrier that should be put on an import is the raising of the price and that it should be raised equally on imports from all sources. The smaller trading countries argued validly that the grey area measures did enough damage to the operation of markets; why legitimize this damage by writing a provision for it into GATT?

This division of opinion remains. The same basic positions are on the table in the Uruguay Round. The European Community is still tinkering with 'selectivity'. In justifying this interest EC officials often confuse two problems: how to deal on the one hand with damaging surges of competitively but fairly priced imports and how to deal on the other with damaging surges of imports at below cost prices. In the second case, if it is proved that the exporter is dumping then GATT rules permit an anti-dumping duty to be placed on that import from that country. But if dumping and damage cannot be demonstrated then the import is simply too competitive. This is where the GATT safeguards procedures could be used but are not. We are forced to conclude that the European Community is simply looking for a way to legitimize protectionist inclinations.

Selectivity is strongly opposed by countries in the Asian pacific region and by other efficient textile and agriculture exporters. There is a direct link between the operation of these procedures and negotiations in other areas. If there is agreement to begin liberalizing areas of trade which have been heavily protected, especially agriculture and textiles, there will be a need for arrangements to allow temporary protection against import surges for industries which had previously been sheltered from competition. This is what the safeguards provisions were originally intended to do. It is very unlikely that a fundamental departure from this most basic of GATT principles will be agreed in the negotiations. There may be agreement to reduce the onerousness of the conditions to be satisfied before temporary barriers could be sanctioned.

For many GATT watchers and trade commentators revival of US and EC commitment to the safeguards mechanisms is the touchstone of GATT's revival. They might be right. It is the Holy Grail. The acid test is whether the United States, the European Community and Japan – which has as willingly contrived in these trading arrangements as the other two – are prepared to phase out the existing arrangements. US officials are now starting to complain more loudly and more publicly that they would prefer Japan to cease exercising voluntary restraint on the export of automobiles to the United States. What began as a US initiative has become a Japanese initiative. The United States has also stated that if other countries, i.e. mainly the European Community join it, it will phase out the quotas with which it regulates the import of steel from every country which is competitive. This would be a start.

While important, the safeguards question is not one of the matters of political controversy in the Uruguay Round. Substantial agreements in the four most contentious areas – agriculture, services, intellectual property and textiles – would in themselves be so important that this would reinvigorate commitments to the GATT system. Preparedness to apply GATT rules in trade in textiles and agriculture would be a significant shift away from the use of grey area measures.

The basic issue in the safeguards negotiations is not whether or not deficiencies in the existing GATT rules can be corrected. Some minor changes can be made. The issue is whether the United States and the European Community want to behave differently.

Opening markets

For all the complication and legalisms, the underlying issue in multilateral trade negotiations is whether or not agreements lead to markets being opened to all comers. In the early GATT negotiations the mechanism was to lower tariffs. As a result of past negotiations tariffs are not significant trade barriers in most industrialized countries. From the trans-Atlantic perspective of GATT the tariff negotiations in the Uruguay Round are unimportant. This has led to a common overstatement among commentators that the tariff negotiations are not important and that the only measure of success of market opening in the Uruguay Round would be agreement to reduce the incidence of non-tariff measures.

This overlooks the fresh importance of the GATT system to many developing countries. Tariffs are high among developing countries as compared to the industrialized world, notably among the developing countries which are liberalizing and basing growth on trade. As these countries seek to gain greater access to the markets of the industrialized countries they are being challenged to lower their tariffs and bind them to GATT rules, the key commitment being to agree not to raise tariffs again in the future. As part of the Uruguay Round many developing countries, including all the significant traders, have agreed to submit data to the GATT tariff database which is used as a basis for negotiations to lower tariffs. This important development has passed largely unnoticed by academic GATT commentators.

This is not to say that the industrialized countries will not be participating in the tariff negotiations. They will. If the mountains of paper setting out available offers for reduction are any guide, these will be protracted and complicated negotiations. And in each industrialized country there are sensitive sectors in which tariffs are higher than average.

Individual negotiating groups were established for each tariff measures and non-tariff measures. This was something of a structural mistake. Virtually every non-tariff measure that exists was covered already in another area of the negotiations. The incidence of these measures is great in the textiles and agriculture sectors for which there are separate negotiating groups. Many grey area measures are covered in the safeguards groups. And there is a separate negotiating group to deal with subsidies which is the other significant generic non-tariff measure. There is little to be achieved in the non-tariff negotiating group other than to exhort a reduction of the incidence of non-tariff measures and perhaps to monitor efforts in other areas.

Some commentators have cast an uneducated eye over the work of the non-tariffs group and deduced that the lack of substantive activity in it indicates that non-tariff issues are not being tackled in the Uruguay Round. They have looked in the wrong place.

Proposals to reduce the incidence of non-tariff measures have become part of the tariff negotiations as well as part of the work in the other negotiating groups. A novel feature of the tariff negotiations is that proposals to reduce or eliminate specific non-tariff barriers have been advanced as companions to proposals to reduce tariffs where a non-tariff barrier impedes the item of trade under discussion. The United States has forced the pace on this. The logic is unchallengeable. The point of securing a tariff reduction can be significantly undermined if there is a non-tariff barrier in place which still impedes trade.

But the US action raises a significant point of principle. It was invoked early in the negotiations against suggestions that, instead of having separate groups to negotiate on tariffs and non-tariff measures, a single group be set up for negotiations to improve market access. The idea was that this group would cover both tariffs and non-tariff measures. This was strongly opposed. Most non-tariff measures are not legal under GATT rules and members of GATT are under a standing obligation to eliminate them. Because tariffs are legal, credit can be claimed for offers to cut them. To mix up reductions of tariffs and non-tariff measures might lead to claims for credit for cutting illegal measures.

By acting as they have, however, the Americans will ensure

that there is a degree of joint bargaining to reduce both tariff and non-tariff measures. The Americans have practicality on their side if they do not have principle. Negotiators will always indignantly protest when offered a reduction in a non-tariff barrier that they cannot be expected to give credit for the offer since the measure was not legal under the GATT. Nor should they ever do so. Sometimes however, it can make another offer look sweeter.

Chapter Fourteen
FIXING GATT –
new markets

One of the many aspects that gives the Uruguay Round its unique character is the aim of extending into other sectors of the global economy the GATT precepts of market competition and trade rights. These new areas of trade are services, intellectual property and investment. Grafting these areas on to the GATT system, especially services, will build a basis for global growth in the future as much as will opening up the areas of trade which have always been within GATT's scope but have been actively excluded.

Services – new trade

A General Agreement on Trade in Services (it is already being described as GATS) will be a product of the Uruguay Round. This could have a far greater effect on international business over the next three decades than is generally imagined if the negotiators show foresight. The idea is to apply free trade principles and the model for open trade which apply in GATT to international trade in services.

International rules which govern trade in services already exist; but these are not rules which foster competitive trade or open economies. The general characteristic of international agreements governing air transport, shipping, and telecommunications is that they enable businesses which usually enjoy some monopoly over a national market to barter over shares of international business. The cost of transmitting data globally, an air ticket or shipping space is fundamentally determined by agreements between governments about how much business the carrier concerned is allowed to conduct. Only within those limits is there some competition on the price of the product.

GATS would set out common international trade rules to apply over time to all international transactions. The basic laws would require signatories to make regulations and the process of preparing them transparent; to extend any opening of a market to any other signatory; and to accept an international system of dispute settlement.

These new rules would not apply to all services transactions from the day the agreement opened for signature. This would not be realistic. There is very heavy regulation of significant services sectors. A process of gradual liberalization like that which operated in GATT is envisaged. When countries sign the agreement they will furnish lists of particular activities to which they do not intend all or some of the new rules to apply. For example, all are expected to exempt air traffic rights. Many will exempt certain banking activities.

The agreement will provide for progressive liberalization. It is probable that not long after the end of the Uruguay Round, and every few years after that, an international conference will be held where countries will negotiate to reduce the number of exempted areas. Over time the free trade rules of the agreement will gradually extend to more and more activities, opening up markets.

A key issue is whether or not the agreement would cover every single service transaction. The European Community wants this, as does the US administration. However, there are pressures to exclude specific sectors from the agreement. In the United States the US shipping industry is lobbying strongly in Washington to exclude coastal shipping from the agreement. It does not want competition.

The US Treasury is opposed to inclusion of financial services in the agreement. It has been lobbying with other treasuries around the world for support. Its argument in principle is that control of international financial services could not be on the same basis as other areas of activity because financial services transactions are qualitatively different. For example, govern-ments must maintain controls to satisfy the special standards that banks must adhere to, given the consequences of bank failures. However, there is no sound reason why these special interests cannot be satisfied within the framework of an overall umbrella services agreement. What is driving the US Treasury is concern to protect its bureaucratic turf. It has stimulated some similar turf concerns in parts of the European Community.

Similarly, the reservations of the US shipping sector could be met by the administration's reserving the sector of coastal shipping as an area which it did not intend to open up.

It is not tenable for any significant sectors to be permanently excluded from the scope of the agreement. It would unpick if this happened. Once one sector were excluded, governments would find it nearly impossible to reject cases from other sectors for exclusion from the scope of the agreement. This would present a particular problem for the European Community if one member state were able to secure exemption for one sector.

Developing countries are concerned about the umbrella approach. Some continue to harbour reservations about whether they want their services sector to be subject to liberalizing rules at all. Others worry genuinely that they do not have adequate information about the services sectors to be able with confidence to construct a list of activities that they want to initially exempt from the liberalizing obligations of the agreement. Developing countries are also pressing for some recognition of the right to waive the obligations to liberalize, given their special problems. This replicates the position taken by them in GATT over the years. Some general recognition of their problems is likely. There is considerable scope for allowing developing countries to liberalize more gradually than industrialized countries. But formal exemption from the legal obligations of the agreement is unlikely.

Citibank and American Express have been two of the major proponents of liberalization of services. They do not want to see at the end of the Uruguay Round an agreement which simply sets out a theoretical basis for liberalization. They want to see liberalization as well. The concluding phase of the Uruguay Round is therefore likely to witness negotiations to secure some liberalization within the framework of the agreement at the same time as the agreement itself if being finalized.

There will be pressure on the US administration to solicit commitments for the opening up of financial service markets. The US insurance industry can also be expected to press for the opening of insurance markets. Under pressure from it the United States has used its 301 muscle to gain access to foreign markets. The European Community also wants early action to liberalize financial services. It will press its trading partners to offer to match the wider financial services market that the single market programme is creating in the Community. The Community has warned that it will seek reciprocal openings of markets for the increased access that non-EC banks will be able to enjoy.

The telecommunications companies in Europe and the United States want markets for value-added services opened up. There is tacit consent that existing monopoly rights which exist in most countries should remain in place for the early years of the agreement at least. There is a long-term trend of deregulation of basic telecommunication services and open competition in these sectors. Technology has already demonstrated that there is no difference between a domestic and international telecommunication service. The European Community is also interested in opening up opportunities for aircraft servicing and port and harbour services.

Labour is a large export service for a number of developing countries. A number of them have indicated that they will press for greater opportunities to export labour. There is no theoretical difference between a construction worker and an architect except what they charge for their services. However, countries, including developing countries, are not likely to subsume their immigration laws to a GATS.

The relationship of the negotiations on services to the rest of the negotiations will arise. The major concession that the developing countries secured at Punta del Este was that the services negotiations would be formally delinked from the rest of the negotiations. This issue matters most in assessing the value of trade concessions. Under GATT if a tariff binding on the import of tractors is breached, the exporting country concerned has a theoretical right to seek compensation through the adjustment of a trade barrier on any other item of trade between the two countries.

They developing countries would argue that the agreement at Punta means that it would not be possible to introduce concessions granted in services negotiations into this system. Given the breadth of traded services it would seem an unnecessary complication to seek to do so. It would appear that some industrialized countries have not given up on the idea of cross-linking trade concessions in the goods area with trade concessions in the services area. If they wish to get developing country support for this it will cost them.

The major threat to the services negotiations is ironically posed by interests in the industrialized countries which are the primary proponents of liberalization. Businesses which dominate trade do not regard it as normal to give opponents full opportunities to compete. British banking favours the liberalization of services. Go into the City, however, and there is palpable lack of enthusiasm for making an effort to open up an area which is regarded as under full control.

This gives rise to the risk that the services agreement might end up with the effective result of a deal between the European Community and the United States, and maybe Japan, to set up a framework in which they give each other greater market access but do not set up an agreement which is trade liberalizing. What is wrong with this is what is wrong with oligopolies. The level of competitiveness is regulated and not driven by the market and trade is rigged to the interests of those who control it.

This is the fundamental difference between an agreement that allows the most competitive operator to set the standard which the market recognizes or one that allows established operators to negotiate shares of access into each others' markets. Apprehension about introduction of competition guided policy makers in Canada, Switzerland and the Nordic countries to toy at an early part of the Uruguay Round negotiations with the concept of expanding trade through reciprocal exchanges of negotiated access to markets rather than by increasing the exposure of domestic markets to global competition. They were driven by fear of the competitive power of their major trading partners. But it was an approach that would be contrary to their own long-term interests.

The second danger is pressure to accommodate short-term interests. The full benefit of a GATS may not be experienced for

10 to 20 years. Yet powerful sectional interest groups, like the US coastal shipping industry, will be concerned to avoid any arrangement which threatens the protection of their industry, now or in the future. There will be a temptation to the negotiators to concede specific exclusions in order to secure a short-term benefit for another industry, in the US case say for American Express. The long-term consequence could be to fatally flaw the agreement. Constituencies in governments for the long view are weaker and even less numerous than the constituencies for liberalization.

A final strategic threat to negotiation of an effective, liberalizing services agreement is the European Economic Space. This is the arrangement which is to enable the EFTA countries to participate in the new European single market. The services industries in many European markets are protected. Getting access to the markets of the European Community/European Economic Space may be the limit of ambition of internationalizing trade in services for these countries. This may lead to a positive disinclination to see an agreement which encourages global markets.

This agreement will succeed if the powerful industries in the industrialized world perceive that it is in their long term interests to lay out arrangements that will encourage competition, and if smaller traders insist that the fundamental principles of liberalization in the agreement are effective. Such an agreement will optimize the prospects for global growth and reinforce and complement the tide of deregulation that is sweeping the globe.

Intellectual property – trading at the top end

The intersection of intellectual property issues – patents, trademarks and copyright – with international trade has fixed the attention of Hollywood, Christian Dior the pharmaceutical giants and the French wine *negociants* on the Uruguay Round. Agreement on international measures to provide better trading opportunities for products with significant intellectual property components has now become one of a handful of essential results if the Uruguay Round at large is to succeed.

This development is very largely the work of the collective

efforts of the pharmaceutical, recording and information industries in the United States. They have brought considerable pressure on the US administration to elevate intellectual property in its priorities in the negotiations. They have also succeeded in stimulating a strong interest among similar industries in the European Community and Japan.

Through a combination of weak patent and copyright protection and lack of enforcement, mainly in developing countries, these industries claim they lose several billions of dollars per year. Exports of goods with high intellectual property content are also inhibited because cheaper copies and pirated versions of the products undercut the market.

The industrialized countries also argue that unless developing countries have intellectual property rules which provide protection similar to that which prevails in the industrialized world, major companies will be reluctant to invest in or supply their products to developing country economies. They make this point with particular force to the developing countries in the Asian/Pacific region where economic structures are rapidly evolving. This is one of the reasons why there is preparedness by countries in that region to look at the proposals from the big three.

The industrialized countries have proposed that new GATT rules be agreed which will set new standards for intellectual property protection, particularly for copyright, patent and trademarks and provide for enforcement of these as well as established rules in existing international intellectual property conventions. The proposals are ambitious.

The issue is controversial. Some developing countries have established pharmaceutical industries with protected markets to supply cheap, generic rather than brand name drugs and as part of this policy have deliberately weak patent rules. Other countries have significant, powerful domestic industries which flourish in the environment of permissive intellectual property rules.

There is strong opposition from developing countries. The Indian government suffered a strong domestic backlash after concurring even to negotiate on this subject in the GATT. There is a group of developing countries who do not like the idea but are prepared to negotiate, if for no other reason than to deflect the considerable domestic pressure that the United States has been bringing to bear in recent year to improve copyright and patent protection. The ASEAN countries are prominent in this group.

Investment – a long term issue

Countries frequently impose conditions on investment to influence their trading position. Usually the point is to encourage investment in industries to generate exports. Examples are export performance targets and eligibility for tax breaks if investment is in an export sector. Conditions can also be imposed to protect local industry. Common ones are local content rules to require new industries to source a percentage of inputs from domestic industry.

The United States has set out a list of measures which it wants to see proscribed. It does not have much support. The European Community is wary because of the number of measures that are used by member states. Japan is interested in this area. It is now one of the world's major capital exporters. It has financed a great deal of the growth in the Asian/Pacific region. It has also found its investment subject to the sorts of constraints the Americans are objecting to, including in the European Community.

Developing countries are more opposed to GATT rules restraining imposition of trade related conditions on investment than to proposals for an agreement to liberalize services and new rules on trade related aspects of intellectual property. Even among the Asian/Pacific NIEs trade distorting conditions are widely offered or required on investments.

Negotiations will be difficult. Their major significance will be to put this item on the agenda of international trade negotiations for the longer term.

Chapter Fifteen
FREE TRADE –
the challenge of old vices

Protectionism, like taxation, is among the most sensitive of public policies; but unlike taxation protectionism it is easy to increase. It is also easier to cut taxes than protection, as the Reagan administration found. It is one of the paradoxes of the decade that the Reagan administration which was so committed to market forces could not free them more in international trade. Free trade economists have agonized for years about why protectionism is so persistent when the case against it is so clear. Some have even constructed models of behaviour: but politicians never agonize. They understand perfectly why protectionism has appeal and is so hard to reduce. Protection confers benefits on groups. Once a benefit has been conferred on a group in society it does not readily surrender it.

There were fewer advocates of free trade in the business world in the 1980s, particularly in the United States, than in the 1960s or 1970s. And they came from the services industries rather than manufacturing. Nevertheless, in almost all OECD countries recognition is growing that the benefit which is being conferred by protection is basically unearned. A particular need is therefore felt to justify protection and the elaborateness of the justification is usually in direct proportion to the largesse of the protection. The most extreme justifications have been made for protection of agriculture.

Some new variants of protection have emerged in the 1980s, mostly in the European Community and the United States in response to the challenge of Japanese efficiency. The United States has popularized the concept of 'fair' trade. This has been a most successful piece of doublespeak since it has obscured the importance of competitiveness and efficiency. 'Strategic' rather than free trade theories have been toyed with. New techniques of imposing trade barriers through procedural creep and more sophisticated mechanisms for market management have also been developed.

In this environment of trade retaliation and muscle flexing, the demanding of reciprocal concessions reflected the mood of the time. Unilateral liberalization became wimpish in Europe and North America. None of this has altered the fundamentals; as perhaps has been demonstrated by the number of countries in the rest of the world which did choose to unilaterally liberalize their economies in this period. Try as people might to dress things up differently, the basic benefits of efficiency and competitiveness that come from open trade still stand. All the arguments for managing trade and economies differently are basically old wine in new bottles.

Free trade – re-stating the case

Free trade rules perform the same function for international trade as competition laws in domestic economies. The rationale is simple – efficiency. If there are no barriers to trade, products can be imported to be sold if there is a market for them. Increase the price of an import by taxing it – with a tariff – or making it scarce – restricting the number that can be imported by a quota – and the import cannot play its proper role in helping to set a market price.

Economies that are open to all imports receive the cheapest available goods. These will either be the imported good or the domestic good which has been priced to compete with the imported competition. This reduces costs to consumers who then, of course, have more funds available for other purposes. Open economies are also best for countries that want to export. The cost of components will be the world price. This is essential in order to manufacture products for export which are internationally competitive.

The GATT trading system is a rather elaborate means of allowing the most efficiently priced product to help set the market price. It assumes that there will always be someone somewhere who can produce a good cheaper than someone else. This assumption seems well founded. GATT's rules are meant to serve as a bridge between the best priced goods in various domestic markets, not a barrier. The tariff is the only barrier encouraged by GATT. It allows a clear distinction to be set between the prices of imports and domestically produced goods. The international market price will be the tariff free price in any country. This enables any country to quickly establish its international competitiveness.

The other critical aspect of the GATT trading system is that it does not allow a distinction to be drawn between goods of the same type from different countries. This is consistent with the point that it is the price, and only the price, of the good that matters. Also consistent with this, GATT requires that any reduction of tariff on an import from one country has to be extended to imports from all countries.

The liberal economics of the GATT system remain the most efficient means of conducting international trade and promoting growth. Where the system does not appear to deliver the goods it is because the participants concerned are not prepared to apply its principles. The more the principles are disregarded the lower is the optimal rate of global growth that can be achieved.

The most rational action to take is the one that is often the hardest to sell – to liberalize and deregulate unilaterally. If so, why bother to participate in the GATT system? The reason is that when other countries liberalize and they are in the GATT system, they are obliged to do it so that other members of the system get some of the benefit as well. The benefits of liberalization are spread.

This is not abstract theory. The United States could use a falling tariff rather than expanding quotas to open its steel market. Not only would US manufacturers like Caterpillar be able to buy cheaper steel, but more members of GATT – Brazil, Poland and the European Community – would have greater opportunities to compete on price in the US steel market. So when individual members of GATT liberalize unilaterally by the GATT rules the rest of the members of the GATT system benefit.

An EC decision to reduce barriers to sugar would enable Cadbury-Schweppes to import cheaper sugar and provide greater export opportunities for sugar growers in the Philippines, Argentina and Australia. In fact one of the complaints of some members of GATT is that some countries gain the benefit of the liberalizations of others and do not themselves contribute. This is said mainly of developing countries.

The full benefit is achieved by the efficiency encouraged. Countries that have greater opportunities to generate income by exporting have more money available to buy imports. As the level of efficiency of production increases, more can be exported and more can be imported.

It was recognized from the outset of GATT that the argument for reducing protection unilaterally within a GATT framework would be difficult to sell to a domestic industry. It would invariably focus on the fact that its protection was going to be reduced. This was one of the reasons for organizing international rounds of trade negotiations where many members of GATT could commit themselves to reduce levels of protection at the same time.

There is a degree of confusion about how the process of exchange of concessions (commitments to reduce tariffs) takes place and to whom the concessions are actually being given. The popular conception of tariff negotiations was that concessions were exchanged reciprocally. This is frequently the language used by the negotiators and sometimes they even calculate the value of the increase in trade which the offer to reduce might achieve to justify why their negotiating partner should offer more. But it is more correct to say that independent agreements to reduce tariffs are entered into simultaneously. This is not just a semantic difference. The fact is that each time one of the partners in a negotiation agrees to a lower tariff they are agreeing to extend that benefit to all other members of GATT at the same time. So GATT members are receiving benefits that they may not know about until the returns are posted at the end of the process.

New bottles – old wine

Reciprocity

Some alternatives to the GATT multilateral system have been popularized over the last decade. Reciprocity is one of the more appealing approaches. Do not liberalize or open markets until others do so and only do it reciprocally – let them into your market only if they let you into theirs is the argument.

Companies in the United States and the European Community suffering pressure from Japanese competitors argue that Japanese imports should only be allowed if Japan allows greater imports from the United States and the European Community. Of course they cannot mean their own products because in most cases they are not competitive. The protectionism behind this line of argument is obvious. The European Community likes reciprocity. It has appeared with ominous regularity as an operating principle in the new rules governing access to the financial services sectors in the single market by companies outside Europe. They may participate in the new single market if EC companies have similar rights of access to the domestic market of the country of origin of the non-EC company. On the face of it the premise of reciprocity – equal exchanges – seems reasonable. Opening markets reciprocally is the line of argument that those arguing for the GATT approach have the most difficulty countering.

The basic flaw of reciprocity is that it does not guarantee that market forces will operate. Reciprocal agreements usually result in the degree of opening being measured by the value of trade which each side secures. It can be achieved by any means and is more likely to be on quantities of trade permitted. The difference from the GATT approach is that under GATT exporters get access to markets if they can meet the price in that market. For the importer that price will be the cost of the cheapest product on the market plus whatever mark up a tariff adds. The process by which the market is opened is to lower the tariff. The greater the cut, the more open the market. Every member of GATT gets the benefit of every other GATT member's tariff reduction.

So the GATT rules protect the market, give all exporters equal opportunities to compete in markets and make markets predictable for business. Access which has been negotiated on the basis of a bilateral deal can easily be altered. GATT commitments cannot easily be altered and the direction and margin of the change is clear to everyone.

If the market is only opened after a reciprocal agreement the extent to which it is opened depends entirely on the bilateral deal. There is no obligation to extend the opening to other importers. The global price mechanism is undermined and so is the competitive pressure that it exerts. The market is undermined. This is always a dangerous basis for business to operate on. Once the price is artificially set it can be artificially set again.

Finally, reciprocity is the way in which the big players can shape markets in their own interest and at the expense of smaller traders. There cannot be reciprocity between a large trader and a small trader. The small trader cannot match the interests of the large trader. The only time reciprocity may work is when each trading partner is of roughly equal weight. Even then, there is no assurance that the deal negotiated recognizes the market. The danger is that the arrangement might be an oligopoly or a cartel. The natural tendency when those who dominate markets get together is to fix prices. We should not expect governments to behave differently from oil companies.

Market management

The greatest damage to international efficiency, and to the international authority of the GATT system, has been done by the market management systems which the United States and the European Community have foisted on Japan and the East Asian economies since the late 1970s. These are the arrangements under which the exporter (mostly Japan) agrees to restrict to an understood figure the number of products to be exported. This can be voluntary. Whether it is or not is not the point.

The consequences can be serious. Always the consumer pays – in the European Community for video cassette recorders, in the United States for automobiles. In addition, there is always a high risk that the protected industry will never adjust but will rescale its cost of production, profits and wages to a market which is insulated from the full competitive effect of the most efficient supplier. This happened to the steel industry in the United States and the European Community as they entered into the spiral of increasingly restrictive trade arrangements beginning in the late 1960s.

Japan has become an unfortunate and willing cooperator in market management. It is difficult to blame the Japanese. In automobiles and electronic goods, the United States and the European Community have consistently offered Japanese industry the opportunities for windfall profits. By encouraging Japanese companies to restrain imports to specified levels, they have enabled Japanese exporters to raise prices since demand for their products was strong. But Japanese industry is not a hapless victim in this. Managing the market seems to come easily to Japanese industry and officials. The level of US exports of semiconductor computer chips to the Japanese market in the mid-1980s remained constant despite variations in the US share of the global market as a result of price and currency fluctuations.

Market management has always had its adherents in the European Community. Throughout the early 1980s the French proposed with regular monotony that the five major wheat suppliers – the United States, the European Community, Canada, Australia and Argentina—agree on market shares for the world wheat market. They were rebuffed, not only on grounds of principle: the timing of the proposal followed a period of sustained exports of subsidized EC wheat on to the international market which had given the Community an historically high share of the global market.

Markets are managed in the clothing and textile sector through the MFA as well as other restraints, and in agriculture where nearly all mechanisms, quotas, voluntary restraint arrangements and orderly marketing arrangements have been used. Japan has recently added to this array of non-market instruments by developing programmes under which Japanese manufacturers are directed to increase imports. It directs its importers to increase the percentage of imports taken from nominated countries with which Japan's trade balance is in surplus. Naturally this includes the United States and most members of the European Community. The effect of these arrangements is likely to be small and it is assumed that Japanese officials and industrialists would wind them back when they found that the competitiveness of industry was affected by requirements not to acquire the cheapest components.

Protection by procedure

One of the weapons developed in the protectionist armoury of the 1980s is procedural protection. Its characteristic is to create rather elaborate bureaucratic procedures which are difficult to follow and which are more rather than less likely to result in a trade barrier being imposed. While most business executives think that all governments work like this these are new phenomena. The European Community has developed its anti-dumping procedures so that they have become effective devices for protection. The United States has established semi-automatic procedures which, once triggered, enhance the likelihood of a trade barrier being imposed.

Anti-dumping – a new European speciality

GATT permits countries to levy duties on imports if the imports are being dumped – sold more cheaply than in domestic or other markets – and are injuring domestic producers. Such a duty may not be imposed wilfully. The dumping and the injury have to be demonstrated. GATT sets out general principles to follow but the means of calculating dumping and the injury which it causes is left to national administrations. There are only four determined anti-dumpers – Australia, Canada, the United States and the European Community. To determine if the product is being dumped requires government officials to do what no one has yet been able to do: artificially construct a market. Each of the four has developed different approaches.

There is no doubt that dumping does occur and that it is an anti-competitive practice. However, there are many instances where anti-dumping procedures themselves have become anti-competitive practices. There is no doubt that in the countries where anti-dumping is resorted to most some sectors of business regard anti-dumping as an instrument of protection, not competition. In 1988 one Australian business representative described anti-dumping as the only instrument remaining to protect industry after tariffs had been lowered. In recession, when industries frequently turn to governments for protection when they are feeling the pinch, there is always also an upsurge of complaints about dumping.

One of the more bizarre justifications for imposing anti-dumping penalties is that it is a source of pressure on the offending government to reduce the incidence of non-tariff measures. This has been argued by EC anti-dumping officials and the case they have in mind is Japan. Of course, whether or not one imported product is fairly priced has nothing to do with whether or not another product exported to the country of origin of the import faces unfair competition. Such confusion about the purpose to be served by anti-dumping investigations may in part explain why procedures have been developed in the way they have and give confusing findings in the way they do.

Anti-dumping has come to be seen as one of the instruments used by the European Community to keep competitively priced products from Japan and the other East Asian economies out. The increase at the end of the 1980s of EC anti-dumping cases against imports from East Asia is striking. Some cases give rise for suspicion about the rationale for the actions, or raise serious doubts about the procedures that have been established.

The Community put anti-dumping duties on video cassette tapes which were manufactured in Hong Kong. These tapes could not have been dumped in the normal meaning of the word. The company did not have a domestic market of any significance with which it could have underwritten sales. It was not operating from the comfort of a sheltered market. Hong Kong is the most open market in the world. Yet the EC procedures found dumping. There is an active debate in Europe about the extent to which EC procedures are constructed, some suggest 'tilted', to make the finding of dumping more likely. In a celebrated analysis in 1988 a British academic, Brian Hindley, demonstrated how in certain cases the Community's methods of calculating dumping by Japanese companies which imported products into the European Community using fully owned subsidiaries would always produce a positive finding because certain marketing and distribution costs were not included when determining the real cost of the imported product.

The Community is not alone. There is an observable trend in the administration of anti-dumping in all of the four major anti-dumpers to tilt the methods of calculation to make the finding of dumping more likely. Japan, Hong Kong and Korea have proposed in the Uruguay Round negotiations that disciplines be introduced to reduce the use of anti-dumping procedures for protectionist purposes. Some minor changes may be agreed. But it is not likely that the United States and the European Community will be stimulated to agree common standards on how anti-dumping will operate until they find their own exports kept out of markets by anti-dumping duties. The time for this is not far off. A number of other countries, including Korea, Turkey, Brazil, Poland and Mexico, are starting to set up their own anti-dumping procedures.

Fair trade – the US rule

The European Community is not the only one to have refined the techniques of procedural protectionism. Each revision of US trade law over the years has introduced more and more criteria by which the trading practices of other countries are scrutinized. Earl Grinols, senior economist to the US Council of Economic Advisers, described the effect of provisions in the 1988 US Trade Act as increasing the number of complaints about foreign trade practices, increasing the likelihood of a decision to intervene, and increasing the size and duration of interventions.

The 1988 Act showed the shift of emphasis to newer forms of protection. It registered only 14 tariff changes and 74 temporary tariff changes, which occupied only 8 per cent of the 482-page act. The main content of the act was procedural changes: it generally enhanced the capacity of the US to deal with 'unfair' trade practices. Unfairness is a relatively new contribution to the language of international trade. Introduced by the United States in the late 1970s, its popularization coincided with the upsurge of protectionist sentiment in the United States in the early 1980s. The competitive Japanese product was never far out of the minds of those who used the expression.

GATT does deal with unfairly priced products if they cause damage. GATT rules are restricted as much as possible to rules which enable the proper price of goods to be seen and, if necessary, calculated. GATT wisely makes an effort to avoid intruding into the area of business practice. And even here its anti-dumping rules are uncomfortable. It is a normal practice for business to take a loss while establishing a presence in a market and winning a market share. This type of activity would be highly susceptible to an anti-dumping finding.

US law, however, has no compunction about identifying practices which go well beyond where the drafters of the GATT drew the line. 'Unreasonable' practices are actionable under US law. These can include measures which deny fair market opportunities to US companies, toleration by foreign governments of systematic anti-competitive practices, and export targeting. The discretion to determine what these mean lies with US officials. The Act also cites denial of worker rights as an actionable foreign trade practice. While this might be a highly commendable concern in its own right, it is as relevant to barriers that impede trade as whether or not the executives of foreign companies run corporate jets.

The 1988 Act broadened the scope of issues upon which the administration was directed to retaliate if the various grounds for offence were established. It narrowed the grounds which the administration might adduce for not taking retaliatory action. The Act also shifted a significant amount of the responsibility for exercising discretion to the US Trade Representative and away from the president.

The Congressional drafters presumably thought that the USTR would either be more susceptible to the blandishments of Congress or that institutionally the USTR would be more inclined to an interventionist approach since the same person would have responsibility for negotiating trade agreements. The administrator of USTR, Carla Hills, has chosen not to exercise these discretions to their full limits. Nevertheless, the 1988 Act consolidates a trend in the United States towards erecting a system of trade retaliation which parallels and can easily go beyond what is allowable in the international system operated by GATT which the administration expects other countries to adhere to.

In 1986 the European Community aped US arrangements for increased discretion to act unilaterally. The creation of this clone invites the opportunity for cycles of retaliation. But this is an option available only to countries with trade clout. There is no point in smaller traders equipping themselves with unilateral powers to retaliate against the trade actions of a bigger trader in addition to their rights to use the GATT. They would always be out-gunned. The more likely effect of the major traders' taking the law into their own hands will be to deter the smaller countries from accepting the open trade disciplines of GATT.

Strategic trade – a theory for the time

In the mid-1980s a line of thinking emerged from some US economists which suggested that the economic precepts of free trade might not be valid and that there were cases where it was feasible for countries to support and protect industry and to achieve a net economic gain. Free trade economists are usually adamant that under no circumstances is there a gain to be achieved from protection. Even if there are exceptional circumstances where this might not be true, such as when one country is the dominant world supplier of one product, free trade supporters usually point out why this situation will not obtain for very long.

Obviously the strategic trade theories were music to the ears of industries and Congress in the United States. Not only might they be a basis for justifying the protection for which they had been pressing, but they could also explain why Japan had become so predominant in some industries, especially since Japan's rate of imports was so low.

The strategic trade theorists have not satisfied these hopes. Most of them concede that the circumstances where protection might generate a net benefit are very specific and atypical. Success would require governments to 'pick winners', something that they have never been very good at. They also concede that the theory does not provide a workable alternative to open international trade principles or GATT arrangements. One must wonder if these lines of thinking would have attracted as much attention if the United States had not maintained its budget deficit for so long.

Trade blocs – optimizing inefficiency

The most popular speculation about alternatives to free trade and the GATT multilateral trading system are trade blocs. Is there a trend to trade blocs? There is certainly a trend to greater economic integration and expansion in the European Community. There are pressures in the long term to extend the North American free trade zone to Mexico. Whether this is good or bad for world trade depends on how much these enlarged groups remain open markets. If they remain open there is no problem. Both can enjoy the benefits of exposure to competitive manufacturing in the rest of the world and their markets can play their role in contributing to global growth.

The catalyst will be the European Community. If it does not keep its markets open and does not ensure that the expanded single market is also accessible to traders outside Europe then the global trading system is likely to fragment around trading constellations. Other possible major constellations are a trans-Pacific trading system or a North American free trade zone and yen bloc economic system. As in the case of the European Community, provided these arrangements keep markets open then the benefits of an open trading system will be retained.

Any of these arrangements would become counter-productive if they made the transition from customs unions or free trade areas to trade bloc by granting preference to products from countries within the group over products from countries outside the group. We can see the sort of features that a global trading system might develop by looking at the situation today with trade in agriculture. If we compare international trade in agriculture to a global trading system, then the CAP is like a trade bloc. It gives preference to produce from other EC countries. Its markets are not open and its producers are insulated from market forces. As a result the Community has a generally very inefficient agricultural sector. It is maintained at great expense by the European consumer and tax payer. International markets are distorted and overall efficiency in the global trading system is impaired. The CAP is an extreme example of a trading bloc, but it demonstrates the consequences of operating a trade bloc within a larger system.

The commitment to introduce market economies in Eastern Europe has encouraged some speculation about a trading group built on greater Europe – extended Community plus EFTA plus Eastern Europe. The fascination with the numbers and the enormity of such a market diverts attention from the practical shortcomings of the idea. Setting those aside, however, a major cost to the global economy would be insulation from each other of the three global centres of high technology – the United States, Japan and Europe. Indeed, if Europe turned its back on the United States and Japan and if there were trans-Pacific collaboration on development of high technology, European industry may decline in levels of efficiency compared with the Pacific. The global efficiencies of interaction between markets across the globe would be lost.

Commentators in the Pacific are increasingly speculating that groups of countries might be better off operating in a regional trade bloc rather than in an imperfectly functioning global trading system. Given that the major impediments to trade are basically barriers imposed by the United States, Japan and the European Community it is hard to see how creation of exclusive trading blocs would make either of them more responsive to opening markets to third countries than the pressure and blandishments to do so which are currently brought to bear through the GATT system.

The only case where countries could achieve increased efficiencies would be if several created a free trade zone and ensured that the average level of access to other trading countries was unchanged.

Free trade areas – half a solution

A network of free trade areas with the United States at the centre of each has been mooted in the past in Washington as a serious alternative to a multilateral GATT system. Presumably what is intended is not that the United States would withdraw from the GATT, but that instead of trying to secure liberalization through GATT and GATT trade rounds the United States would pursue liberalization by creating free trade areas. This is not a better alternative for the United States. It is a global trader. It would gain some benefit from each area created but in most cases the gain would be less than could be achieved by global liberalization through the multilateral system. The exceptions would probably be a free trade area with the European Community or Japan, given the size of US trade with each.

Geopolitics and history rule out a US–EC free trade area. Even so it is instructive to look at the idea hypothetically. Trade barriers between the European Community and the United States are not great, except in agriculture which has been a continuing source of trade friction. The domestic politics of liberalization of agriculture are so vexatious that it is difficult to see either Washington or Brussels committing their farmers to a programme of liberalization of agriculture unless it were part of a global programme.

A free trade agreement between the United States and Japan has been discussed. But we should not overlook the fact that one of the key reasons why the multilateral system has not been as effective as it should be is that the United States has not been prepared to follow its strictures, in particular in its trade dealings with Japan. Why would the United States be better able to handle this by entering a free trade arrangement with Japan?

Chapter Sixteen

THE COST OF FAILURE

A missed opportunity

The Uruguay Round has found itself at a crossroad in history. Because of this, it presents governments with an unparalleled opportunity to revalidate the concept of a multilateral system of international rules to foster free trade. Agreement to a series of measures which will initiate liberalization and renew international commitment to a global system of liberal trading is needed as a critical step in this process. History will record that the Uruguay Round presented that opportunity. It would be one of the great mis-steps in modern history if the opportunity were let slip.

A functioning global, liberal trade system is needed now more than at any time since the GATT system was set up in 1948. The old trans-Atlantic trading order needs buttressing, the new market based Europe needs fostering, the emerging trans-Pacific trading order demands consolidating, the liberalizing developing world deserves supporting and the trends to globalization of markets in good and services need accommodating.

The GATT system has been suffering at the hands of the United States and the European Community and, to a degree, Japan. GATT's utility has been undermined because of illiberal trends in the Community and the United States over the previous two decades. In the industrialized countries commen-

tators and officials have recently toyed with alternative ideas –
trade blocs, free trade areas, limited groupings.

While attention in Europe and North America has focused on
how the big three have disregarded GATT, a trend to liberalization
in the rest of the world over the past decade has been
overlooked. Since the beginning of the decade, countries in
Eastern Europe, the Pacific and in the developing world have
been liberalizing. In addition, the significance of the international
trend to liberalization of services industries in the global trading
system has been overlooked by the trade policy establishment,
except among a handful of negotiators in Geneva and in some
boardrooms around the world. The GATT system needs
revalidating and global trends require fresh commitments to free
trade principles. This process has quietly begun, although this is
not apparent to many observers.

Ignoring the new international imperatives

Economic issues will dominate the international agenda for the
next decade. There are the established issues – managing the
imbalances among the three leading economies, containing
protectionism, achieving sustainable growth in the developing
world, solving the developing country debt problem and
graduating the NIEs. Removal of the cold war from the
dynamics of trans-Atlantic relations adds significant items to
that agenda. The imperative of international relations in Europe
now is to get markets functioning where they are not and to
integrate them where they are.

The challenge before governments is greater integration of
economic management. This is not a new idea. Nearly every
international leader in business or government has made
platitudinous references to global interdependence in speeches
over the past decade or two. What is new is that, over the past
decade, a number of governments have had to move past
platitudes and take economic decisions which have to take into
account developments in other economies and provide for the
effects of their action on other economies. Furthermore, decisions
to surrender sovereignty in the economic sphere have been

taken to shape the conduct of international relations and to address international problems.

Among the group of the seven largest industrial economies there have been efforts to coordinate economic policy for several years. These efforts have had mixed success but they have represented a significant shift from refusal in the past to contemplate such coordination. The first step in German reunification was economic – integrating the currency. And the first step in integrating the unified Germany into the European Community will be monetary union from which will come greater economic cooperation. The structural impediments initiative has led to unprecedented discussions between the United States and Japan over domestic economic management.

These are new international imperatives. A panoply of arrangements will be necessary to meet these needs. Now is the time to rebuild the Bretton Woods system of institutions for managing trade, lending and payments which was set up in the late 1940s.

A forum to review trade issues does not have to be created. It is there in the Uruguay Round. The needs to be satisfied argue more strongly than ever for a non-discriminatory, liberal, international system of trade rules, modernized to meet the needs of changing patterns of trade. A failure to act to consolidate such a system of rules would be to ignore the new international imperatives.

Surrender to myopia

The forces against change are strong. Their interests are traditional – to protect a vested interest. If they prevail and prevent comprehensive liberalization, this would represent a tragically myopic outlook among the governments concerned. Opponents of liberalization in individual countries make a curious international coalition. Among them are US textile and clothing manufacturers, Bavarian pig farmers, the Fiat motor conglomerate, Japanese rice farmers, the Chrysler motor corporation, Brazilian manufacturers, French dairy processors, the large US steel producers, Quebecois farmers, Indian manufacturers, Thai military interests, Portuguese apparel manufacturers, small

Korean farmers, and Philips. This list is not comprehensive or representative. It illustrates the diversity and the parochialism of interests involved. These localized interests argue for no change in their own sector. Many claim to support global liberalization, by which they mean in someone else's industry. Because of the cross-linkages of issues in the Uruguay Round, opposition to liberalization in one of the heavily protected sectors is likely to hold up liberalization in others. The fundamental compact in the Uruguay Round is between those who want the traditionally protected sectors of trade liberalized and those who want new areas of trade liberalized. This was demonstrated at the mid-term review conference at Montreal in December 1988. At its simplest level, if there is no liberalization of agriculture, there will be no liberalization of services. To this mix can also be added textiles and intellectual property.

If opponents of liberalization prevent agreements to liberalize in their own areas of protection, not only will the Uruguay Round fail, but it will reflect a staggeringly myopic perspective on national interest. Consider these examples:

1. Maintaining the small, inefficient German farmer would be more important to the German economy than maintaining international competitiveness in manufacturing.

2. Maintaining outmoded, large steel plants would be more important to the US economy than ensuring competitiveness and vitality in equipment manufacturing industry and opening international financial services markets.

3. Supporting a small, barely viable cheese farmer in the French Alps would be more important than creating markets for the dynamic French telecommunications industry and solving the Latin American debt imbroglio.

4. Maintaining a US apparel worker at several times the cost of putting that worker on full-time vacation would be more important than allowing Bangladesh the opportunity to create sorely needed export industries.

5. Keeping small inefficient rice farmers on the land would be more important to the Japanese economy than programmes

to internationalize it and secure fairer opportunities for investment in other countries of Japanese capital.

None of these are outcomes that governments would rationally opt for. But unless governments accept that liberalization means cutting support for the most protected industries in their own economies, they will undermine their declared policy goals of liberalization.

Trade blocs by default

Geostrategic forces are driving the formation of economic groupings which may evolve into trading blocs. Patterns of trade and economic integration point to the possibility of two or three large aggregations – pan-Europe and either trans-Pacific or Asia/Pacific and North America. Commitments to global liberalization and renewed support for liberal international trade rules would provide a framework within which these tendencies to regionalism could function harmlessly and efficiently. It would encourage the European Community to keep its bigger European markets open to the world, keep the United States committed to multilateralism and focus interest in the Pacific on cooperation rather than preferential trade arrangements.

A large obligation rests on the leaders of Europe. A perception in the rest of the world that Europe might turn its back on it would certainly stimulate formation of other groups in response. There is a deeply held belief in Japan and the Pacific that Europe is already set on this course. It is a case of premature judgement, but it is nevertheless understandable given how manufactures from East Asia have been restrained from entering Europe's markets.

There is no doubt that the best result for everyone would be the completion of the single market as well as global trade liberalization. For the Community this would safeguard against the danger that European industry might turn its back on the world economically, even inadvertently.

The Bush administration has strongly supported multilateralism instead of free trade zones as its preferred approach for the organization of international trade. But US leaders also carry a responsibility not to stampede a rush to trade groupings. Negotiations with Mexico over a free trade pact will re-stimulate anxiety about being excluded from markets which the United States/Canada free trade agreement has generated in Japan and elsewhere. Trans-Pacific trade links raise the possibility of a trans-Pacific trade or economic grouping. The bilateral trade networks across the region are significant. There is a growing consciousness of some sense of common destiny among the countries in the Pacific region. The patterns of Japanese investment in the Pacific region and the rapid growth of intra-Asian regional trade in recent years has also led to speculation about the prospects of a yen bloc.

Among the larger traders in all these groups the global trading interest is sufficiently strong for preferential regional markets not to be a rational, first priority. One quarter of Germany's trade is outside Europe. Japan and the United States both have significant global interests. And the rapidly growing economies in the Pacific region will provide large potential markets for manufacturers and exporters of services in Europe.

In the absence of renewed commitments to global liberalization, tendencies to fragmentation of the global economy will strengthen. This would be one of the great follies of modern times given that markets are globalizing. The first penalty would be constraints on global growth. The international economy would simply function less efficiently. Differences in levels of competitiveness would also widen. This would be the consequence of sheltering industry from the most efficient competitor. Of the various possibilities, one frightening spectre for Europe if the world divided between pan-European and pan-Pacific groupings would be joint collaboration between US and Japanese industry in high technology industries.

Leaving the agriculture morass untouched

Protection of agriculture is a key issue. In the major markets where protection is most intense – the European Community, Japan and the United States – the most extreme form of misallocation of resources can be found. The OECD has estimated that over US$200 billion is transferred annually by consumers and tax payers to farmers in OECD countries. Protection of Japanese, EC and US farmers has repressed prospects for growth in the developing world. Agriculture is a primary source of export earnings for more than half of the heavily indebted countries. With liberalization, important opportunities to increase exports and growth would be created for a number of developing countries.

The economics of food production in many parts of the developing world have also been distorted by agricultural protectionism. Off loading surplus EC and US production in world markets has depressed world prices. This robs farmers in developing countries of the incentive to produce. Food aid is not the enduring solution. At the World Food Conference in Brussels in 1988, Kenneth Kaunda, President of Zambia said that 'Food aid, without assisting us to improve our production efficiencies, equally leads to hunger.'

Until standard GATT rules for international trade apply to agricultural trade it will continue to be a running sore in EC/US relations. Excessive subsidies to farmers in industrialized countries also contribute to environmental pollution. Gro Brundtland, head of the World Commission on Environment and Development, told the World Farmers' Congress in Norway in June 1990 that international agricultural trade had to be liberalized to stimulate food production and reduce ecological degradation. If agricultural protectionism is not reversed, development opportunities for many developing countries will remain stunted, global food production will be retarded, billions of dollars in the industrialized world will continue to be wasted, agricultural trade will remain a source of friction between the United States and the European Community and environmental pollution will continue.

Languishing development

Liberalization of clothing and textiles and agriculture trade is the most tangible action that industrialized countries can take to boost growth in the developing world. It is also 'off the shelf'. No new conceptual work needs to be done or global commissions created to recommend it. It would not solve all problems of development. But it would make a big difference.

The development aspect raises a moral issue. Developing countries, many of which desperately need the income, cannot export their more efficiently produced products to the major markets in the industrialized world. The markets are reserved for the small numbers of inefficient domestic producers. In the case of farmers, they are also heavily subsidized – and most of those subsidies go to a minority of wealthy producers. The public in the industrialized world pay dearly to sustain their inefficient producers (typically twice the price for shirts, three times the price for beef) while developing country producers sustain themselves on dismal or declining standards of living.

Discrimination against exports of clothing and textiles from developing countries is institutionalized. There is less confidence among many developing countries about rapid liberalization of textiles because they have become dependent on guaranteed markets. They continue to support liberalization but on the basis that it should be gradual. Opening markets for clothing and textiles would stimulate significant growth in these industries in major developing countries – China, India, Bangladesh and Pakistan.

Development will languish without liberalization. There is a direct correlation between protection in the industrialized world and growth problems in the developing world. For many countries the struggle to keep economic growth ahead of population growth will be unrelieved unless protectionism declines. In Latin America liberalization is a necessary part of relieving the debt burden. Without it, the prospects are for continued low or negative growth; the longer that continues, the greater becomes the prospect of social unrest and reversion to military rule.

A point perennially made, and worth restating, is that improvement of rates of growth in the developing world would also generate benefits for the industrialized countries. Higher growth makes developing country markets healthier and bigger and offers greater export opportunities for business in the industrialized world. The reverse is also true. For example, the cut in income of the heavily indebted Latin American countries because of the need to service debt has added to the growth of the US trade deficit.

Discouragement of liberalization

It is in the interests of developing countries to opt for open economies. It is in the interest of the rest of the world as well – they will contribute more significantly to global growth if their growing markets are open. Until the Uruguay Round developing countries had not participated actively in the GATT trading system. There has been a significant shift in attitude. It reflects a wider trend towards the introduction of market mechanisms and liberalization of domestic economies in the developing world. There is general acceptance among developing countries that if there is a liberalization which benefits them it is reasonable that they should contribute to that process in one way or another in the negotiations.

An effective, liberal trading system is particularly important for the Eastern European economies and the rapidly growing economies in the Pacific. Governments need all the help they can get when they liberalize. An international rule or commitment under GATT can sometimes be enough to overcome domestic resistance to change or resist pressure for more protection. The Eastern European markets need the buttressing that the GATT system can provide.

Over the next decade, Asian/Pacific economies face difficult decisions to modernize their economies, particularly reducing trade barriers and deregulating financial sectors. They have a choice. For some like Korea it is between liberalization or a semi-managed economy on the Japanese model of growth. For others it is between an efficient economy and an inefficient economy. GATT can reinforce these difficult decisions.

The GATT system has to be credible, however, and demonstrate that it works for all. The industrialized world has to demonstrate that the system will no longer be stacked against developing countries. Commitments to liberalize agriculture and clothing and textiles are critical. If they are not made there is no basis for efforts by industrialized economies to encourage liberalization in the developing world. If GATT is not revitalized, the trends to liberalization apparent in the Pacific rim, in parts of Latin America and in Eastern Europe may lapse and reverse.

Retarded growth

Despite exclusion of significant sectors of trade from the GATT liberal trade rules, world trade itself has continued to expand. So the system is not dead on its feet. This expansion has occurred in the areas of trade conducted in accordance with GATT rules as well as in some of those which are heavily controlled, particularly certain manufactures – clothing and textile exports from Hong Kong and Korea, electronic exports from Japan and Korea and automobile exports from Japan. We know that in these areas there would have been greater trade if the restrictions had not been there.

Nevertheless the drift to managed trade is dangerous. It is principally practised between Japan and the United States and Japan and the European Community. The traditional pattern had been for Japan to restrain exports in response to overtures from Europe and the United States to curtail exports. It has recently begun a new practice of stimulating imports by tax concessions and setting import targets for Japanese companies to meet. At first glance this may seem good – it should help to reduce the imbalances of trade between Japan and the United States and the European Community. But it has the same short-term effect as imposition of voluntary imposition of limits to exports. The market is not allowed to operate, fundamental competitiveness is not restored or established.

Commitments to multilateralism by the big three are necessary to arrest this trend. They have shown greater preparedness since the Uruguay Round began to utilize more and respect the processes of the GATT dispute settlement procedures. An overall result from the Uruguay Round towards global liberalization would strengthen support for multilateralism.

A failure to do so would probably accelerate the trend to managed trade. The consequences of this would be progressive reduction of efficiency in the global economy as well as in domestic economies. At the time when companies are starting to operate on a global basis and perceive the need for the global markets without impediments government would intensify its interference with the operation of these markets.

Lost efficiencies

Expanding the definition of international trade to encompass services and creating a GATT for services are far-sighted actions. They anticipate the advent of the Information Age. At an international conference for national coalitions of services industries in May 1990 Arthur Dunkel commented that the pioneering character of the work being done in negotiating a new agreement to liberalize trade in services reminded him of GATTs own modest beginnings in 1948. Like GATT then, a services agreement now could significantly contribute to economic growth in the future.

The effort to develop rules for the liberalization of trade in services is one of the rare occasions in international life when development of an international regime is running apace with market forces rather than being led by them. There is a significant trend to domestic deregulation of services. The European Community is well advanced in opening up internal services markets as part of the Single Market. International trade in services will grow rapidly. The driving forces – telecommunications and financial services – themselves are being driven by the dramatic increases in efficiency made possible by information technology.

A successful agreement could in time stimulate significant efficiences in global economic activity and could as a result indirectly boost rates of global growth. The fate of negotiations over services is intertwined with the outcome of negotiations in the traditional areas. A failure in the Uruguay Round would mean a General Agreement on Trade in Services would not come into force in 1990. This would incur a significant opportunity cost.

Nipping in the bud

Much of the rhetoric and conventional wisdom about GATT in the 1970s and the 1980s has not been adjusted to take into account what has happened in GATT since the Uruguay Round began. The prevailing view is that the GATT system is in bad shape. Non-tariff measures are as prevalent as ever. The United

States, the European Community and Japan are as merrily managing trade as ever.

A number of developments have take place which do not suggest that the GATT system is dying or even comatose. They point to its coming to life.

1. Membership of GATT is increasing. Countries which joined in the last few years include Mexico, Morocco and Tunisia. China is re-negotiating its status. Eight countries are negotiating accession. Saudi Arabia, the USSR, Taiwan and Laos have all expressed interest in joining.

2. A number of important trade disputes have been brought into the GATT dispute settlement system for resolution by the big three – opening of the Japanese beef market, aspects of the disputes over the semi-conductor trade, the US/EC oilseeds trade dispute, and the dispute between Japan and the European Community over screwdriver assembly.

3. The Uruguay Round is the most complex trade round mounted. It is running to schedule and has delivered interim results from the negotiation. The most important was the agreement to give GATT the power to examine systematically the trade policies of parties to GATT. This is a major addition to its established functions.

4. Negotiations are proceeding to establish rules for entirely new sets of activity. The very concept of what is traded has already been dramatically expanded by the work on services. Significant extensions of the jurisdiction of GATT – intellectual property and investment – are being considered.

5. Significant trade liberalization has occurred since the Round began. Japan's decision to open its beef market will, by conservative estimates, increase beef imports to Japan over a five to six-year period by US$2 billion. This was achieved as a result of US bilateral pressure, but the United States (and Australia and New Zealand) also used GATT procedures and the result was according to GATT principles. Agricultural cases are now a normal part of the GATT disputes processes. This was not the case a decade ago.

GATT is gradually reviving. Failure to get substantive results in the Uruguay Round would therefore be the more damaging. It would nip in the bud a promising revival. This would be more devastating and damaging to the multilateral trading system than a nil result in a static environment.

The challenge of free trade

The arguments for the benefits of free trade and the case for a strong, global, liberal trading system to promote them are as pertinent as ever. In addition the Uruguay Round has found itself at one of the crossroads of history. The decisions taken in it can be as important for the development of the trading system in the next fifty years as the bearing on the trading system over the last forty years of the decisions taken at the first GATT conference.

The primary challenge is to establish multilateral trading principles as the reference points for international trade into the next half century. Given geopolitical forces, this will be difficult. On the other hand the price to be paid – lower optimal growth, constrained development, lower food productivity, continuing tension over trade issues, disruption of a natural tendency to evolution of global markets – is reason enough to succeed in a rational world. But if we had a rational world we would not have the inefficiencies of protection. The challenge of free trade is for governments to think clearly. The challenge of the Uruguay Round is for governments to recognize the extent of its importance and act to realize it.

Appendix 1

THE CHRONOLOGY OF THE URUGUAY ROUND

June 1985
Informal meeting of trade ministers in Stockholm discusses possible trade round including the problem of services.

September 1985
Special Session of GATT Contracting Parties establishes a committee to prepare for a multilateral trade negotiation.

February 1986
Seoul informal meeting of trade ministers.

July 1986
Informal negotiations in the EFTA building over a draft communiqué to launch the trade round.

Completion of the work of the preparatory committee for the ministerial meeting at Punta del Este.

August 1986
Inaugural meeting of the Cairns Group in Northern Australia.

September 1986
Ministerial meeting at Punta del Este to launch the Uruguay Round of multilateral trade negotiations. Meeting agrees general objectives for the Round and sets four-year deadline.

January 1987
Trade Negotiations Committee establishes the 16-committee struc-

ture of the negotiations, appoints presiding officers, agrees negotiating plans.

March 1987
Informal trade ministers meeting at Lake Taupo, New Zealand.

Clayton Yeutter floats concepts of mid-term review of the Round to secure interim results.

July 1987
Venice Summit of the big seven endorses the need for progress in the Round and the importance of the negotiations on agriculture.

December 1987
Informal deadline for tabling of most of the first round of negotiating proposals basically met.

February 1988
Trade Negotiations Committee decides to hold a mid-term review of the trade round in Montreal in December 1988.

April 1988
Informal meeting of trade ministers in Konstanz, Germany reviews progress in the Round.

October 1988
Informal meeting of trade ministers in Islamabad previews the Montreal meeting and reaches informal consensus on issues to be covered in the mid-term review.

December 1988
Mid-term review of the Round held in Montreal. Preliminary agreements reached to liberalize tropical products markets, improve dispute settlement procedures, improve functioning of GATT, settle the framework for a services agreement and to aim for 30 per cent reduction in tariffs.

Meeting adjourned until April because of failure to agree on agriculture.

April 1989
Agreement reached on negotiating objectives for agriculture and other issues left unagreed when Montreal meeting broke – intellectual property, textiles and safeguards.

June 1989

Trade Negotiations Committee decides that the final ministerial meeting to conclude the Round would be held in Brussels in December 1990.

October 1989

Informal meeting of trade ministers in Tokyo.

April 1990

Informal meeting of trade ministers, Puetro Vallarta, Mexico.

July 1990

Group of seven summit in Houston endorses the importance of agricultural reform in the Uruguay Round.

Trade Negotiations Committee adopts frameworks for outcomes at the final Brussels meeting.

October 1990

Informal trade ministers' meeting in Italy previews Brussels meeting.

December 1990

Meeting of ministers to negotiate final results and conclude the Uruguay Round, Brussels.

Appendix 2
DRAMATIS PERSONAE

Andriesson, Frans
Vice-president of the European Commission – responsible for agriculture until 1989, thereafter responsible for external relations and trade.

Arnell, Lars
Swedish ambassador to GATT in Geneva and chairman of the Uruguay Round negotiating group on intellectual property.

Brock, Bill
Former US senator and US Trade Representative until the end of 1984.

Dawkins, John
Australian Minister for Trade 1985–86.

de Clercq, Willy
European Commissioner for external relations and trade 1986–89.

de Zeeuw, Art
Chairman of the Uruguay Round negotiating group on agriculture.

Duffy, Michael
Australian Minister for Trade Negotiations 1987–89.

Dunkel, Arthur
Director-General of GATT and alternate chairman of Trade Negotiations Committee.

Field, Peter
Deputy-secretary, Australian Department of Foreign Affairs and Trade.

Girard, Pierre-Louis
Swiss Ambassador to GATT, 1984–88.

Gradin, Anita
Swedish Minister for Trade.

Hills, Carla
US Trade Representative, 1989–.

Iglesias, Enrique
Managing director, Inter-American Development Bank, Uruguayan Foreign Minister and chairman of the Punta del Este ministerial meeting 1986.

Jaramillo, Felipe
Colombian ambassador to GATT, chairman of the Uruguay Round negotiating group on services.

Katz, Jules
Chairman of the Uruguay Round negotiating group on the functioning of GATT 1987–88, deputy USTR 1989–.

Kobayashi, Tomohiko
Chairman of the Uruguay Round negotiating group on trade related investment measures.

Lacarte-Muro, Julio
Uruguayan ambassador to GATT and chairman of the Uruguay Round negotiating group on dispute settlement.

Lyng, Richard
US Secretary for Agriculture 1985–88.

Moore, Mike
New Zealand Minister for External Relations and Trade.

Smith, Michael B.
Deputy USTR Washington until December 1988.

Tettamanti, Leopoldo
Argentine ambassador to GATT.

Tran Van Thinh (Paul)
Representative of the European Community to GATT.

Yeutter Clayton
USTR 1985–88, Secretary of Agriculture 1989–.

Zerbino, Ricardo
Foreign Minister of Uruguay and chairman of the Montreal ministerial meeting 1988.

Appendix 3

THE BUSINESSMAN'S GUIDE TO GATTspeak

The quick guide to GATT jargon

GATT – The General Agreement on Tariffs and Trade. An international agreement which commits countries to free up trade. Sets out international rules and creates trade rights.

Contracting party – legalese for GATT member. Lawyers love to point out that countries do not 'join' the organization, but become 'parties' to contractual obligations in the Agreement.

MTN – multilateral trade negotiations. A discrete conference held every five to seven years to negotiate global reductions to trade. Also known as trade rounds. Can run for several years marooning officials in proximity to the Swiss ski slopes.

Uruguay Round – name given to the multilateral trade negotiations begun in 1986 because the conference which initiated it was held in Uruguay.

Multilateral trade principles – longhand for GATT principles. International fair competition and anti-monopoly rules. Contrasted by bilateral trade deals which invariably distort international markets and disadvantage third parties.

Golden GATT rules – there are nearly forty articles in GATT as well as other associated codes and agreements. There are a handful of very basic rules which are at the heart of the GATT. These are all you really need to know:

MFN – most favoured nation principle. Every GATT party gets the best treatment available. When a market is opened to one GATT party it has to be opened to all other GATT parties.

Non-discrimination – a product imported from one GATT party has to be treated in the same way as the same product from another GATT party.

National treatment – imported products must be treated like domestic products.

Prefer the tariff – Gatt rules oblige countries to use tariffs to restrict imports. Quotas may be used only in restricted cases.

Binding – countries are encouraged to bind their tariffs at designated levels to make reductions in protection non-reversible.

Dumping – parties are not permitted to export products at prices lower than the price in domestic markets if this damages the interests of local manufacturers in the export market.

Safeguards – the procedures under which GATT parties are allowed to raise barriers against a sudden and damaging flood of fairly priced imports to give the threatened industry time to restructure. Not much used – too stringent for the United States and the European Community. Usually an eye glazer to explain – see glossary.

Non-tariff measures – A substantial amount of international trade is governed by restrictions which are not sanctioned under GATT. Most common are VRAs (voluntary restraint arrangements). These were usually restraints on the volume of exports to the European Community and the United States applied voluntarily by Japanese industry after informal suggestions by EC or US officials that this would be neater than being bludgeoned under domestic law.

GATT council – Steering body for the GATT. Meets every six to eight weeks, mainly to hear, process and adjudicate trade disputes.

TNC – Trade Negotiations Committee (steering body for the Uruguay Round).

The meaning of GATT articles
(or how to hold your own at a GATT cocktail party)

GATT delegates and officials like their work and like to talk about it. They especially relish talking about the articles of GATT to which nearly every issue can be related. Most can in fact talk in 'articles' which seem like riddles to the uninformed. As a result few other people talk to them except other delegates and officials.

In case you would like to show some erudition or impress your local GATT representative at a GATT cocktail party, the following is a guide to the more important articles.

Article I
The most favoured nation article – one of the golden GATT rules.

Article II
The non-discrimination article – another golden rule.

Article VI
A favourite in certain circles in Brussels, Washington, Ottawa and Canberra. Permits levying of anti-dumping duty providing damage (not so popular) is found.

Article XI.2.(c).i
Very dear to the hearts of Canadian dairy farmers, but not Canada's Cairns colleagues. A complex provision that allows imposition of quotas to restrain agricultural imports.

Article XIII
One for the connoisseur. Does not permit discrimination in the application of quotas.

Article XIV.6
Does not exist. But if you suspect your interlocutor is showing off or knows less than you do, casually mention it and check the response.

Article XVI.4
Allows export subsidies on primary products. Export subsidies are otherwise not permitted on other products. Will ingratiate yourself with US delegates if you make clucking sounds about this article.

Article XVIII
Highly valued by developing countries – allows them to impose trade barriers to manage adverse balances of payments. Regarded by many

industrialized countries as abused. Careless comments can cause arguments. Be careful.

Article XIX

Another one for the connoisseur – the safeguards provision. Make disapproving noises about 'grey area measures' and 'selectivity' (see glossary) – unless it is an EC party in which case you should do the reverse.

Article XX

The national security clause. Show off – the article the United States used to justify its trade embargo against Nicaragua.

Article XXIII

Sets out procedures for GATT dispute settlement. To 'take an Article XXIII action' is to initiate a complaint about another country's trade measures. This is the one the Americans should use instead of Section 301 (see glossary).

Article XXIV.6

Sets the conditions that a customs union or free trade area should satisfy to stay within GATT bounds. Many delegations believe it is a long time since the European Community satisfied these terms. Be careful about wisecracks. You will quickly find the limit of the sense of humour of EC delegates.

Article XXVIII

Sets out rights and procedures for negotiating tariffs. Arcane. Never allow yourself to be caught in a conversation between two Article XXVIII experts.

Part IV

Not an article, but several provisions which set out the entitlement of developing countries to 'special and more favourable treatment'. Bigger bark than bite. Also sensitive.

Appendix 4

GLOSSARY OF URUGUAY ROUND TERMINOLOGY AND TRIVIA

Anti-dumping
The lawyer's favourite. This is the area of GATT law in which the professionals brings the full processes and expense of the law to bear. If after investigation an import is found to be selling below its domestic price and damaging industry in the importing country, the authorities may levy an anti-dumping duty. The greatest incidence of anti-dumping investigations and penalties is found in the United States, the European Community, Canada and Australia.

ASEAN
The Association of South-east Asian Nations – Brunei, Indonesia, Malaysia, the Philippines, Singapore and Thailand.

Binding
To bind a tariff is to agree to bind it to GATT rules, in particular not to raise it. This is usually done during a round of trade negotiations in consultation with other parties with whom the original deal to lower the tariff was struck and/or a party who is the principal supplier of the product concerned. Each party to GATT has a tariff schedule. In it is recorded the bound tariffs. Once so recorded these schedules become a formal part of the terms of accession of each party to GATT. Once a tariff is bound it may not be raised. However, if a party wishes to raise the tariff it is obliged to consult with other parties, particularly those with whom the lower tariff level was bound.

To agree to bind tariffs in the schedule is one of the generalized commitments that parties to the GATT can make as a contribution to the process of multilateral liberalization. One of the objectives of the

United States and the European Community in the Uruguay Round is to get countries whose average levels of binding was low to bind more tariffs. 89–90 per cent of tariffs in industrialized countries are bound. The norm among developing countries is much lower.

CAP – Common Agricultural Policy

The CAP is the European Community's system of agricultural support and protection.

Centre William Rappard

The name of the building in which the GATT secretariat is located and the organization meets in Geneva.

Dispute Settlement

Clayton Yeutter always listed improvements to the GATT's dispute settlement procedures as one of the United States's key targets for the Uruguay Round. It was one of the areas nominated by the administration from which early results were to be achieved. Improvements to the procedures were agreed at the mid-term review of the negotiations in Monteal in December 1988. The major effect is to tighten up the timetable for the process and put time limits on how long each step in the process is allowed to last.

At least two key issues fundamental to the authority of the GATT system remain on the table, however. One is to strengthen fundamentally the juridical character of the system and separate the interests of plaintiff, respondent, jury and judge. The other is to separate judgments on legality from decisions about implementation. The United States has proposed that when the outcome of a panel is brought to the GATT council for decision, the complainant and the defendant should not participate in the decision. This would involve a significant further transfer of sovereignty to the GATT from parties to it.

It would probably be the only basis upon which the administration could argue to Congress that a significantly strengthened system such as this would warrant surrender of the powers under the US Trade Act to deal with trading partners unilaterally. The European Community is ambivalent about this. It has shifted from its trenchant opposition of the past to the idea. It is focusing on two approaches. The first is to introduce procedures in which a decision about whether a measure was illegal would be separated from what action should be taken to correct it. The Community argues that corrective measures should be negotiated. It has indicated willingness to consider the US approach in tandem. To those who prefer the more legalistic approach, the EC approach raises questions about whether scope for bargaining over the corrective measure might diminish existing requirements to make the measures consistent with GATT. The second EC tack is to put pressure on the United States to relinquish powers like that in Section 301 of the US Trade Act. It has skilfully over the last few years exploited disenchantment among other parties to GATT over the exercise of these powers by the United States. The United States has a powerful bargaining tool in the negotiations if it is prepared to put relinquishment of these powers on the table.

European Community
Two arms of the Community play a role in trade negotiations. The European Commission represents it in negotiations. Commission negotiators are usually accompanied by the member state which is currently the president of the European Council.

EFTA
European Free Trade Association. Members are Austria, Finland, Iceland, Norway, Sweden and Switzerland. This organization is in danger of extinction as more and more members toy with the idea of joining the European Community.

FOGs
Functioning of the GATT system. One of the negotiating groups in the Uruguay Round was given this inelegant appellation. It was from this negotiating group that the system of surveillance of the policies of GATT parties emerged. Countries agreed to these proposals at Montreal. A recommendation from the group that every second meeting of the annual session of the GATT contracting parties (the GATT annual meeting) should be attended by ministers was also adopted. This provided for the first time a forum in the GATT where ministers could meet regularly. (The informal meetings of trade ministers – see entry – are not official GATT meetings.)

Free trade areas (FTAs)
These areas are created when countries agree to eliminate all trade barriers among themselves. This is a technical transgression of the GATT principle that members of the GATT are supposed to lower trade barriers equally to all other GATT parties. GATT permits free trade areas if the average tariff levels of the countries of the area are not higher after the free trade area comes into effect. There are few real free trade areas.

The most significant free trade areas exist among the EFTA countries, between Canada and the United States, between Australia and New Zealand and among South Pacific Island countries and Australia and New Zealand (SPARTACA). There are others, but they vary in the extent to which all barriers to trade are eliminated.

GATT articles

This is the title of one of the Uruguay Round negotiating groups. It was a catch all group to pick up issues related to an article to which any participant might have wanted to propose a change. A major issue considered in this group was the extent to which developing countries could impose trade barriers to manage adverse balances of payments. (Article XVIII). The United States and the European Community believed these rights should be curtailed. There was trenchant opposition from developing countries. Proposals were also made to alter the way in which trade rights set out under Article XXVII were created and modified.

GATT ministerial

Shorthand for the ministerial meeting of GATT parties held in 1982. Widely regarded as an unsuccessful meeting. The failure of this meeting is what stimulated US officials to begin to push for the Uruguay Round and to toy with the idea of free trade areas. Held at the nadir of the recession, this meeting bears out the author's view that liberalization can usually only be achieved when there is growth and governments have the room to manoeuvre which they need to manage restructuring. This is not the view of many economists who like to argue that times of crisis are the times to introduce radical change. Many governments have found themselves with major political problems after taking advice from economists on how to manage changes to public policy.

Gitane

Arthur Dunkel's preferred cigarette.

Globality

It was basic to the Community's support for the Round that there be globality. All issues were linked and negotiations to liberalize one sector could not proceed without parallel negotiations in all others – especially agriculture. The concept always seemed more natural in French *globalité*.

The green room

The green room is in the executive annex of the GATT building, near Dunkel's office. The painted surfaces are cream, but around the wall is a khaki green wallpaper panelling. It has an oval table which would normally sit 18 comfortably. The room is large enough for another row of 20 seats around the wall for seconds. The Green Room is where problems are thrashed out.

All work is conducted in English. GATT has a business like tradition. Formality supposedly has no place. But the conference world in Geneva encourages the worst in diplomats and many cannot shake the habits of circumlocution.

Occasionally the essential function of a diplomat, which is to be a cipher for the government, is confused with the formality of being a representative of the government. The result is that some representatives start to behave as if they are the government; which means that things inevitably take longer. Some diplomats from the former British sphere of influence who have been posted to Geneva for long periods have even been known to effect the British royal we when referring to themselves.

The green room has an air conditioner but only on one side of the room. The non-smokers tended to sit on the upwind side of the table. It is difficult not to see your neighbour's negotiating brief when you sit next to him for hour after hour. It is likely that the location of the air conditioner has affected the type of agreements reached over time in the green room.

Grey area measures

Measures which are claimed by those who use them to fall into a grey area of GATT legality. The users contend that GATT may not sanction them directly but they have not been demonstrated in the GATT as being illegal. Non-users are nearly unanimous in their view that grey area measures contravene the GATT's market principles and clearly should not exist. Examples are orderly marketing arrangements and voluntary restraint arrangements. A recent creature has emerged which has been called the voluntary import expansion (VIE). This is used to describe targets for increased imports which Japanese officials now set for some companies in Japan.

Group for Negotiations on Goods (GNG)

An umbrella group to which the various negotiating groups dealing with all issues but services reports. The group is superfluous: it simply retransmits the results from the various negotiating groups (except services) to the TNC. It was created as part of the deal at Punta to ensure that negotiations between the goods and services area of the negotiations were formally separated. (see Figure 11.1).

Group for Negotiations on Services (GNS)
The negotiating group in the Uruguay Round for services.

Informal trade ministers' meetings
Until it was agreed at the Montreal mid-term review that every two years the annual meeting of the GATT contracting parties should be attended by ministers there was no formal occasion where trade ministers would meet regularly. In 1983, Bill Brock convened the beginning of a series of informal meetings of trade ministers. There is a common core of about 25 countries which attend, but the host of the meeting is at liberty to invite others. The meetings were held initially at yearly intervals, but as the Round approached and then began, meetings were held about every six months.

These meetings became important for ensuring that ministers regularly focused on the issues and the state of affairs in the negotiations. Before the Round was launched meetings were held in Washington, Brazil, Stockholm, and Seoul. After 1986 there were meetings in Taupo (New Zealand) in 1987, Konstanz (Germany) and Islamabad in 1988, Tokyo in 1989, and Puerto Vallarta (Mexico) and Italy in 1990.

Intervention
Intervention is Geneva terminology for a statement. The GATT is free of some of the more tedious pomp of the UN. Flowery and gracious statements of thanks to the previous speaker no matter how offensive, inoffensive, perspicacious or pointless the statement may have been is *de rigueur* in the UN but not GATT. Discussion is comparatively direct. Nevertheless, a certain amount of coded language is used. At one point during the Uruguay Round negotiations a guide to the use of phrases was circulated privately – less for the edification of delegates than for their amusement (see Figure A.1).

National Submissions to Negotiating Groups

- 'I have referred the paper back to my capital.' (I haven't read it but perhaps they will.)
- 'A comprehensive submission.' (It's over 2 pages in length and seems to have an awful lot of headings.)
- 'An interesting paper.' (I don't want to rubbish it yet./I really don't quite know how to deal with it.)
- 'An ambitious proposal.' (It is unlikely to get any support.)
- 'An innovative proposal.' (This one really is out of the trees.)
- 'The paper is unbalanced.' (It does not contain any of our views.)
- 'This proposal strikes a good balance.' (Our interests are completely safeguarded.)
- 'I'd like to make some preliminary comments.' (I feel that I must say something but it won't be worth reporting.)
- 'We will be making detailed comments at a later stage.' (Expect that your posting will be over before you hear from us.)
- 'I should like to make some brief comments.' (You have time for a cup of coffee.)
- 'I'd like to make some personal comments.' (My capital won't agree with me.)
- 'This paper contains some interesting features.' (I'm going to give you some face-saving reasons why it should be withdrawn.)
- 'I will go through and make comments on individual points.' (This is an opportunity for me to read the paper and for those of you that haven't read it, to listen.)
- 'The proposal is outside the terms of the ministerial mandate.' (I want to stop this proposal immediately.)
- 'I am gratified by the support for our paper.' (Thank God at least one delegation did not rubbish it.)

Secretariat papers

- 'I'd like to thank the Secretariat . . . ' (Why not, the paper is no worse than any other.)

FIGURE A.1 *'What they said' (what they really meant)*

- 'The paper will provide useful background to our discussions.' (I haven't read it.)
- 'I'd like to make some comments.' (I have read the paper and I don't like it.)
- 'I'd like to make some detailed comments.' (My capital had apoplexy over the paper.)

Transparency

- 'In the interests of transparency.' (This has already been agreed by those who count.)
- 'We need transparency in the process.' (I'm worried that I won't be included in the back-room negotiations.)
- 'We believe that transparency throughout this exercise has been good.' (The few selective bits of information we made available appear to have done the trick.)

General

- 'This subject is dealt with in another negotiating group.' (We won't look at it there, either.)
- 'Our position is evolving.' (We have started to think about the issue now and could go in any direction.)
- 'We agree with the views of . . . ' (I don't understand what the discussion is about . . .)
- 'English is not my mother tongue.' (I am about to give you a lecture on a fine point of syntax.)
- 'The delegate of . . . spoke eloquently on this subject.' (I haven't got the faintest idea what he means.)
- 'I am not sure that I fully understand your point.' (I know exactly what you are saying and I don't agree.)
- 'I was sent here to negotiate.' (Be prepared for some stonewalling.)

Special category

- 'I have not read the paper but I like it.'

FIGURE A.1 *continued*

MFA - Multi-Fibre Agreement

This is the formal agreement by which imports of textiles and clothing from developing countries are restricted by the industrialized country members of the agreement.

MTN

Multilateral trade negotiations. Abbreviation of round of multilateral trade negotiations which is technically what each trade round is (see Table 1.1).

MTN agreements and arrangements

This was also the title of a negotiating group in the Uruguay Round. It was created to encompass all the codes and agreements which were negotiated in the Tokyo Round. The most controversial issue in this complex has been the anti-dumping code. The East Asian economies, particularly Japan, Korea and Hong Kong are pressing for changes to the anti-dumping code to restrict the degree to which arbitrary interpretation of the code and Article VI of the GATT occurs to allow anti-dumping procedures to block imports.

Natural resource based products

This category basically includes non agricultural primary products, i.e. minerals, metals, lumber and fisheries. A negotiating group was created for it. Major exporters have worked hard to gain attention to problems of trade in this area but not with much success. Trade problems include escalation of tariffs as the exported product moves further up the processing chain away from the primary product export and subsidization of domestic extraction of a mineral product such as coal, to the cost of competitive imports. In a hangover from the Arab oil embargoes of the 1970s the European Community uses this negotiating area to press for assurances of supply. This area of the negotiations is not likely to lead to much, despite the efforts of Australia and Chile.

Newly industrializing economies (NIEs, also NICs)

These are the high growth developing countries who can see within reasonable periods of time that they will achieve OECD standards of living. In the 1970s they were newly industrializing countries. As well as South Korea, Taiwan, and Singapore they included Brazil and Mexico. The Latin American debt problem has led people to cease including the Latins in the list. Because of Hong Kong's spectacular economic performance, and because it is not an independent country, the concept of newly industrializing economy has been coined to include Hong Kong. Thailand and Malaysia are regarded as candidate members of this category.

Combine any phrase from Column I with any phrase in Columns II, III, and IV and you will obtain a universal GATT statement. The number of possible combinations is 10,000. You will be able to speak for about 40 hours.

Column I	Column II
Mr Chairman,	the introduction of effective disciplines and compliance with existing rules
There is evidence to support our view that	the further development of multilateral trade co-operation
In these circumstances it is our position that	a realistic attempt to curb the rising protectionist pressures
As my distinguised colleagues have rightly noted	a continuous improvement in the North-South trade relations
In addition,	a balanced and pragmatic solution of the current debt crises
My government is convinced that	a rapid reduction in the bilateral trade imbalances
Many contracting parties share our opinion that	a constant search of mutually satisfactory arrangements on trade in services
Recent developments in trade policy clearly show that	a full implementation of the objectives stated in the ministerial declaration
My delegation is of the opinion that	a long-term solution to the proliferation of grey-area measures
Neither should we forget that	a balanced attempt at solving the issue of safeguards

FIGURE A.2 *Universal GATT speech*

Column III	Column IV
should play a significant role in	the reinforcement of the GATT system
ought to be given a prominent place in our current efforts aiming at	a more co-ordinated attempt to address the global economic problems
requires serious consideration of various proposals directed at	changing the negative trends characterizing the present state of affairs
would provide a valid contribution to the urgent task of	strengthening the non-discrimination principle of the international trading system
calls for an energetic action with a view to	assuring a further liberalization of international trade
is one of the major elements of a successful strategy aiming at	creating an atmosphere of mutual confidence and understanding among the major parties concerned
necessitates a resolute action on the part of all trading nations targeted at	implementing the standstill and rollback commitments
requires that substantial progress is also reached in other areas which are essential for	assuring more stability in the field of trade and finance
should be given a proper place in negotiations directed at	avoiding the constant deterioration of the trading environment
consititutes a *sine qua non* for	resolving the current tensions in the trading system

FIGURE A.2 *continued*

Punta del Este
Charming beach resort east of Montevideo where the Uruguayan government hosted the ministerial meeting at which agreement to launch the Round was reached.

Quadrilaterals
In the mid-1970s, when trade tensions among the United States and the European Community and Japan began to threaten to become broader bilateral problems, the trade ministers of those three administrations as well as Canada started to meet privately to provide a forum where difficulties could be discussed frankly to ensure that the problems were managed.

During the Tokyo Round this forum became something of a steering group for those trade negotiations. This was resented by other countries. To appease other industrialized countries, the big four agreed to begin regular consultation with other key industrialized countries. Some wit from the big four dubbed the forum 'the eight dwarfs'. It expanded over time to include all industrialized countries and is now inelegantly dubbed the 'dirty dozen'. This title was bestowed by the US ambassador of the time, Michael Samuels. The quads maintained their forum and it has met roughly at half-yearly intervals during the Uruguay Round. The meetings are informal, led by ministers and not too structured. They have used the forum carefully and have avoided allegations or complaints that it is a steering group: but sometimes it is.

Safeguards
GATT shorthand for provisions to allow emergency trade barriers to be put in place to 'safeguard' a domestic industry against a surge of highly competitive imports. These are permitted under Article XIX of the GATT. To maintain faith with GATT's commitment to the market, the barriers must be imposed equally on all imports and commitments need to be entered into to phase the measures out – they are meant to be imposed to allow the uncompetitive industry breathing space to restructure and regain competitiveness. These conditions have been too painful for the United States and the European Community to follow and they have disregarded the provisions and resorted to grey area measures.

Secretariat
The GATT secretariat numbers about three hundred all up. As international organizations go, this is lean. The average calibre of their officers is high and commitment is high. No one should complain at

proposals to increase the staff of the secretariat after the Uruguay Round.

There will be a significant range of additional functions to perform. The greatest tribulation for secretariat staff is to have to accept as serious virtually all proposals from delegates, no matter how silly.

Section 22 waiver
This is the formal waiver which the United States won from the GATT in 1955 to exempt some of its agricultural trade from GATT rules. It was generally regarded as a temporary measure. The United States has put it on the table in the Uruguay Round.

Section 301
That part of the US Trade Act which mandates the administration to act unilaterally to redress trade problems. Very unpopular with other members of the GATT.

Speeches
Diplomats are not noted for their inventive use of language, especially in speeches. Most of their time preparing speeches is devoted to ensuring that the point they want to make is perceived, or not perceived too strongly or with luck not perceived at all. A significant body of cliché exists which most diplomats draw on to fill out their speeches, to obscure the point of their speeches or simply because they are lazy.

A long suffering soul, probably a member of the GATT secretariat who has been tortured for years (see secretariat) having to listen to intervention after intervention by delegates, collated the most regularly used phrases and clichés. They can be rearranged in any number of combinations to produce the all purpose GATTspeech. (see Figure A.2).

Subsidies
For an instrument that emerged from a process of negotiation, the various provisions of GATT are very consistent. Its edicts to trade and to use trade barriers in a way which preserves the market price as a reference point support the objective of reinforcing and opening up markets; with one surprising exception. GATT is remarkably permissive on the use of subsidies. Only the use of export subsidies (and then only in the case of trade in manufactures) is prohibited. Otherwise countries are generally enjoined to avoid use of subsidies if it damages the interests of trading partners.

Yet a government subsidy can be paid to support the manufacture of a product which enables it to be sold at a price in a domestic market and undercut an import. This can be as effective a trade barrier as any of the more conventionally recognized barriers. The OECD has started some pioneering work to assess the extent to which subsidies are paid to industry in the industrialized world.

The negotiations to reduce protection in agriculture recognize fully that domestic subsidies are an integral part of the machinery of protection. Nevertheless, most countries in GATT defend subsidies as a right – which they undoubtedly are – but peculiarly few see their importance as a trade barrier. The concept that trade is an activity relevant only to activities outside one's borders is economically irrational. However, even in GATT it has its adherents.

A code was negotiated during the Tokyo Round to tighten the conditions under which subsidies might be paid and to clarify the condition upon which countervailing duties may be levied on subsidized imports. Few countries joined it. The United States and Canada have made proposals in the Uruguay Round to strengthen rules restricting the use of subsidies.

One of the major issues is how to define a subsidy. The United States introduced its proposals on the need for greater GATT constraint on subsidies only half way through the Uruguay Round. The negotiations have focused on an American idea to differentiate between subsidies which are allowable, those that are definitely not allowable and those that are in between. They are colloquially referred to by colour. The red subsidies are not allowable, green are permissible. Some agreement refining the different types of subsidies is likely.

Swiss protocol
The terms by which Switzerland acceded to GATT. Notable because Switzerland negotiated with nearly all members of the GATT to exempt its agriculture sector from GATT rules.

Trade Negotiations Committee (TNC)
Executive body directing the Uruguay Round. Composed of all the countries participating in the Round. Presided over by the Director General of GATT when meeting at the level of officials and the foreign minister of Uruguay (as hosts of the launching of the Round) when meeting as ministers.

UNCTAD
The United Nations Conference on Trade and Development. Not a conference at all but a permanent organization based in Geneva. It is an integral part of the UN secretariat. UNCTAD reflected strongly a view of development which was fashionable in the 1960s and 1970s but has not yielded results. The organization is having trouble adapting to the changing world.

BIBLIOGRAPHY

American Enterprise Institute for Public Body Research, *Global Competition in Financial Services: Market Structure, Protection, and Trade Liberalization*, by I. Walter, The American Enterprise Institute Trade Services Series, Competing in a Changing World Economy Project, Ballinger Publishing Company, Massachusetts, 1988.

American Enterprise Institute for Public Body Research, *When Countries Talk: International Trade in Telecommunications Services*, by J. D. Aronson, and P. F. Cowhey, The American Enterprise Institute Trade in Services Series, Ballinger Publishing Company, Massachusetts, 1988.

Balassa B., *Subsidies and Countervailing Measures: Critical Issues for the Uruguay Round*, The World Bank discussion Papers, No. 55, The World Bank, Washington DC, 1989

Balassa B and Noland M., *Japan in the World Economy*, Institute for International Economics, Washington DC, 1988

Bergsten C. F., *America in the World Economy: A Strategy for the 1990s*, Institute for International Economics, Washington DC, 1988

Bureau of Agricultural Economics Canberra, *Agricultural Policies in the European Community: Their Origins, Nature and Effects on Production and Trade*, Policy Monograph No. 2, Australian Government Publishing Service, Canberra, 1985.

Burstein, D., *Yen! The Threat to Japan's Financial Empire*, Bantam Schwartz, in association. Transworld, Sydney, Auckland, 1989.

Centre for International Economics Canberra, *Macroeconomic Consequences of Farm Support Policies*, Duke Press Policy Studies, eds. A. B. Stoeckel, D. Vincent and S Cuthbertson, Duke University Press, Durham and London, 1989

Clarke W. M., *Planning for Europe: 1992 – Britain and the Common Internal Market*, Waterlow, London, 1989.

Cline W. R., *The Future of World Trade in Textiles and Apparel*, Institute for International Economics, Washington DC, 1987.

Emmott, B., *The Sun Also Sets: Why Japan will not be Number One*, Simon & Schuster, London, 1989.

Finger J. M., *The Uruguay Round: A Handbook for the Multilateral Trade Negotiations*, The World Bank, Washington DC, 1987.

Hamilton C. B., *Textiles Trade and the Developing Countries: Eliminating the Multi-Fibre Arrangements in the 1990s*, The World Bank, Washington DC, 1990

Hudec R. E., *Developing Countries in the GATT Legal System*, The Trade Policy Research Centre, Thames Essay No. 50, Gower Publishing Company, UK, 1987.

Iacocca, L., *Iacocca: An Autobiography*, Bantam Paperback Edition, Bantam Books, New York (with W. Novak), 1984.

International Trade 86–87: General Agreement on Tariffs and Trade, Geneva 1987.

International Trade 88–89: General Agreement on Tariffs and Trade, vol. 1, Geneva, 1989.

International Trade 88–89: General Agreement on Tariffs and Trade, vol. 2, Geneva, 1989.

Jacobson, J. and Hillkirk, J. *Xerox: American Samurai*, Macmillan Publishing Company, Canada, 1987.

Jones, K., Politics vs Economics in World Steel Trade, *World Industry Studies*, No. 4, ed. I. Walter, Allen & Unwin, London, 1986.

Kennedy, P., *The Rise and Fall of the Great Powers: Economic Change and Military Conflict from 1500 to 2000*, Random House, New York, 1987.

Kostecki M. M., *East-West Trade and the GATT System*, Macmillan, London, 1979.

Office of the United States Trade Representative, *1990 National Trade Estimate Report on Foreign Trade Barriers*, U.S. Government Printing Office, Washington DC, 1990.

Pelkmans J. and Winters L. A., *Europe's Domestic Market*, Chatham House Papers No. 43, Routledge, London (with H. Wallace), 1988.

The Trade Policy Research Centre, *Has the Cavalry Arrived?: A Report on Trade Liberalisation and Economic Recovery*, by a Study Group under the Chairmanship of B. Scott, Special Report No. 6, Trade Policy Research Centre, London, 1984.

Tussie, D., *The Less Developed Countries and the World Trading System: A Challenge to the GATT*, ed. S. Strange, Printer Publishers, London, 1987.

United Nations, *Trade Routes to Sustained Economic Growth*, Report of a

Study Group of the Trade Policy Research Centre under the Chairmanship of A. Viravan, Tokyo Trade Symposium to mark the Fortieth Anniversary of the United Nations, Macmillan Press, London, 1987.

Van der Wee, H., Prosperity and Upheaval: The World Economy 1945–1980, *The Pelican History of the World Economy in the Twentieth Century,* ed. W. Fischer, translators R. Hogg and M. R. Hall, Penguin, Middlesex, 1987.

INDEX

Geographical expressions are inverted where appropriate, e.g. 'America, Central'.
Countries are indexed without inversion. Germany is treated as one unit.

DATE DUE

NOV 2 5 1993			
GAYLORD			PRINTED IN U.S.A.